Lynda McGraw

PRECISION-PIECED QUILTS
USING THE FOUNDATION METHOD

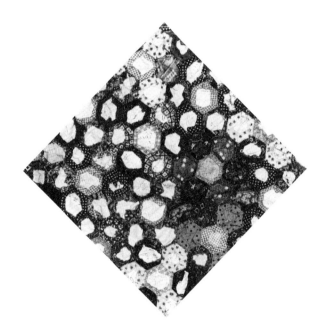

PRECISION-PIECED
QUILTS
USING THE
FOUNDATION METHOD

JANE HALL &
DIXIE HAYWOOD

CONTEMPORARY
QUIL*TING

Chilton Book Company
Radnor, Pennsylvania

Published in Radnor, Pennsylvania 19089, by Chilton Book Company

Color photographs by Jack Mathieson and Jim Conroy, except as noted
B&W photographs by Robert M. Hall and Robert C. Haywood
Illustrations by the authors
Computer illustrations by Rosalyn Carson
Designed by Anthony Jacobson

Manufactured in the United States of America

Library of Congress Cataloging in Publication Data

Hall, Jane.
    Precision pieced quilts : using the foundation method / Jane Hall
and Dixie Haywood.
        p.   cm.—(Contemporary quilting)
    Includes bibliographical references and index.
    ISBN 0-8019-8330-4. — ISBN 0-8019-8329-0 (pbk.)
    1. Quilting—Patterns.   I. Haywood, Dixie.   II. Title.
III. Series.
TT835.H3322   1992
746.9'7—dc20   91-76425
                                                    CIP

1 2 3 4 5 6 7 8 9 0   1 0 9 8 7 6 5 4 3 2

OTHER BOOKS AVAILABLE FROM CHILTON
Robbie Fanning, Series Editor

Contemporary Quilting Series

Contemporary Quilting Techniques, by Pat Cairns
Fast Patch, by Anita Hallock
Fourteen Easy Baby Quilts, by Margaret Dittman
Machine-Quilted Jackets, Vests, and Coats, by
    Nancy Moore
The Quilter's Guide to Rotary Cutting, by Donna
    Poster
Scrap Quilts Using Fast Patch, by Anita Hallock
Speed-Cut Quilts, by Donna Poster
Teach Yourself Machine Piecing and Quilting, by
    Debra Wagner

Creative Machine Arts Series

ABCs of Serging, by Tammy Young and Lori
    Bottom
The Button Lover's Book, by Marilyn Green
Claire Shaeffer's Fabric Sewing Guide
The Complete Book of Machine Embroidery, by
    Robbie and Tony Fanning
Creative Nurseries Illustrated, by Debra Terry and
    Juli Plooster
Creative Serging Illustrated, by Pati Palmer, Gail
    Brown, and Sue Green
Distinctive Serger Gifts and Crafts, by Naomi
    Baker and Tammy Young
The Expectant Mother's Wardrobe Planner, by
    Rebecca Dumlao
The Fabric Lover's Scrapbook, by Margaret
    Dittman
Friendship Quilts by Hand and Machine, by
    Carolyn Vosburg Hall
Gifts Galore, by Jane Warnick and Jackie Dodson
How to Make Soft Jewelry, by Jackie Dodson
Innovative Serging, by Gail Brown and Tammy
    Young
Innovative Sewing, by Gail Brown and Tammy
    Young
*Owner's Guide to Sewing Machines, Sergers, and
    Knitting Machines*, by Gale Grigg Hazen
Petite Pizzazz, by Barb Griffin
Putting on the Glitz, by Sandra L. Hatch and Ann
    Boyce
Sew, Serge, Press, by Jan Saunders
Sewing and Collecting Vintage Fashions, by Eileen
    MacIntosh
Simply Serge Any Fabric, by Naomi Baker and
    Tammy Young
Twenty Easy Machine-Made Rugs, by Jackie
    Dodson

**Know Your Sewing Machine Series,
  by Jackie Dodson**

Know Your Bernina, second edition
Know Your Brother, with Jane Warnick
Know Your Elna, with Carol Ahles
Know Your New Home, with Judi Cull and Vicki
    Lyn Hastings
Know Your Pfaff, with Audrey Griese
Know Your Sewing Machine
Know Your Singer
Know Your Viking, with Jan Saunders
Know Your White, with Jan Saunders

**Know Your Serger Series,
  by Tammy Young and Naomi Baker**

Know Your baby lock
Know Your Pfaff Hobbylock
Know Your White Superlock
Know Your Serger

**Teach Yourself to Sew Better Series,
  by Jan Saunders**

A Step-by-Step Guide to Your Bernina
A Step-by-Step Guide to Your New Home
A Step-by-Step Guide to Your Sewing Machine
A Step-by-Step Guide to Your Viking

Jane dedicates this book to
her ever-patient family,
especially her husband, Bob.

———————

Dixie dedicates this book to
Jean and Hope,
with whom she first shared
the benefits and joys of collaboration

Contents

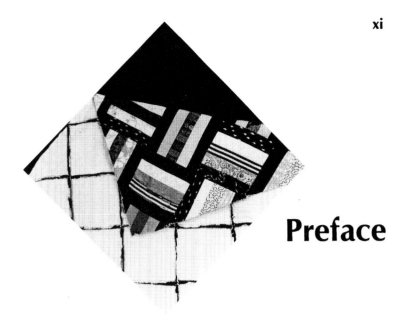

Preface

After we wrote *Perfect Pineapples*, it became clear to us that piecing on foundations had more application for today's quilter than the single pattern we explored in that book.

A foundation is an additional layer used as a base on which to piece. This extra layer is used either to stabilize the piecing or to define the piecing pattern, and is completely covered by the pieces. A foundation can vary in size from a patch or segment, to a block or even to an entire quilt. It can be permanent or temporary. It can be made of a variety of materials, pieced onto by several methods.

Working on a foundation makes it easy to achieve precision. It also adds the stability that is needed when using hard-to-handle fabrics or fabric cut off-grain to take best advantage of a pattern. It can be a valuable design tool. These features of foundation work are useful whether you are making a favorite traditional pattern or a complex innovative design.

This book explores foundation techniques for pieced quilts that a quilter at any skill level can use. In addition, we provide detailed directions for piecing five blocks and ten small quilts, so that you can sample these techniques with a variety of design categories.

It is important to us as teachers to give our students a firm foundation of basic techniques. It is equally important for us to give them the knowledge and the confidence to extend the boundaries of these techniques in their own way. We believe foundation work has a valuable place in a quilter's repertoire, so that she can draw from the widest base of techniques to achieve her personal vision.

Again, we continue to find collaboration rewarding, productive and entertaining. We each bring to this our individual approaches but our philosophy is unified.

We would like to thank those who offered encouragement and advice. We are particularly grateful for those quilters who have generously given of their time to assist us with the "Getting Started" wall quilts in the design sections. Each of them is well-known for her special technique and their contributions have made this a more stimulating book. We thank those who graciously shared their quilts with us for the Gallery. And, last but not least, we thank our students, past and present whose enthusiasm lifts and pushes us as teachers and authors.

PRECISION-PIECED QUILTS
USING THE FOUNDATION METHOD

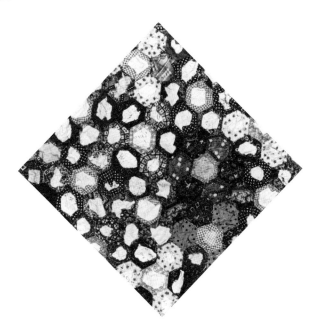

CHAPTER 1

Introduction to Foundation-Based Piecing

Quilters in the United States have made pieced quilts using foundations for well over one hundred years. The foundations were generally in block form for pressed-piecing in such patterns as Log Cabin, String, Pineapple or Crazy piecing. Mosaic-like patterns, where template bases defined shapes such as hexagons or diamonds, predated these block-based quilts.

In other parts of the world, foundations were used much earlier. In England, there is documented Log Cabin foundation piecing dating from the 17th Century[1] as well as Mosaic quilts from the early 18th Century.[2] In Japan, with its tradition of reverence for fabric, there is documented patchwork dating from the 8th Century, made by arranging bits of silk onto a foundation.[3]

Jane found this pillowtop (Figure 1-1) in a Korean Folk Village outside of Seoul, where she was told it is an ancient traditional Korean pattern. It is made of narrow brightly-colored ribbons stitched onto a foundation of interfacing in a pattern that we know as Pineapple.

Figure 1-1. Korean silk pillowtop.

In Central Asia, the nomadic people of the Uzbek region produced Koraki. This is press-pieced patchwork using small triangular and square shapes, heavily imbued with personal and religious symbolism.[4] In fact, some of the designs on a Koraki camel flank hanging (Figure 1-2) are exact duplicates of quilt patterns we consider American patchwork (Figure 1-3). We would not be surprised to find foundation-based piecing in other cultures as well, since it is such a practical technique.

developed primarily from the need for a stable piecing base. The necessity of utilizing scraps of precious materials of varying sizes, shapes and grain lines, and the desire to make these scraps into patterns, made foundations an appealing tool. The resulting precision in the finished piece surely was a welcome benefit.

The fabrics in early foundation-based quilts include cotton, linen, silk and wool, sometimes in the same quilt (Figure 1-4). The quality of these fabrics varied enormously even when the same fiber was used throughout. For instance, cottons could range from expensive imported chintz to loosely woven domestic cloth. In addition to the quality, the property of a fabric such as silk, satin or velvet could make a stable base an important consideration.

Figure 1-2. Koraki camel flank hanging, from the collection of Adolf Siegrist, Basel, Switzerland

Figure 1-4. Detail of antique Pineapple quilt, showing silk, taffeta, cotton and wool strips in the same block.

Figure 1-3. Wild Goose Chase block, duplicating Uzbek Koraki.

Many, if not all, of the patterns commonly pieced with foundations have also been made in the same time period without a foundation, using a running stitched seam. The use of foundations

It is clear why foundation blocks were used for Crazy piecing and String blocks, where the quilter basically was creating fabric from small irregularly shaped pieces of material. Foundations solved other stability problems as well. In center-based patterns such as Log Cabin and Pineapple, the blocks could be kept flat and consistent in size, even with the distorting tendency of piecing around a center. These foundations were sometimes marked in an attempt to provide greater accuracy. In addition, it is apparent from examining antique quilts that the fabric was often used with little regard for the straight of the grain, making a stable foundation even more useful.

The designs in which single template foundations were used are more complex, involving multiple sides and points such as diamonds, hexagons, parallelograms, and rhomboids. These mosaic-like designs contained the same variety of fabrics, but in addition were often cut from more difficult-to-handle fabrics such as silks (Figure 1-5). They too, were often cut with skewed grain. With a stabilizing template, matching points and intersections was simple and accurate.

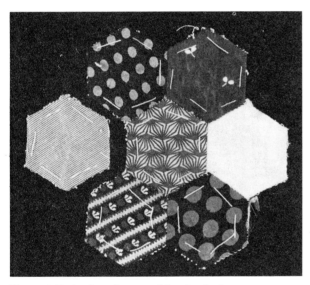

Figure 1-5. Antique hexagon Mosaic piecing.

For today's quilter, these same considerations are valid. Fabric can be created; hard-to-handle fabric can be used; and complex designs, whether traditional or innovative, are possible. In addition to stability, accuracy and precision can be built in by marking the pattern onto the foundation. With these new approaches to the use of foundations, piecing can be made easier for children, inexperienced beginners, and those of us with sight problems, arthritis or other physical disabilities.

Today foundation work has evolved, with a wider choice of foundation materials, several piecing options, and new applications for their use. In the following chapter we will discuss the materials and techniques. Subsequent chapters will explore design categories, and present some small projects that will get you started trying familar patterns with new techniques or, perhaps, using new techniques to try patterns and ideas that you thought were beyond your level of skill.

References

1. Janet Rae, *Quilts of the British Isles* (London: Bellew Publishing, 1987) 68
2. Rae, 52
3. Jill Liddell and Yuko Watanabe, *Japanese Quilts* (New York: E.P. Dutton, 1988) 5–10
4. Schnuppe von Gwinner, *The History of the Patchwork Quilt* (Munich: Keyser Book Publishing Ltd., 1987) 37–39.

CHAPTER 2

Foundation Materials and Techniques

Foundation-based piecing can be constructed in three basic formats: block, segment, or piece. Many patterns use a combination of one or more of these formats.

Formats

Block

Quilters are most familiar with the square block format, probably because of the popularity of String, Crazy, Log Cabin, and Pineapple patterns. These patterns are covered individually in Chapters 3, 4, or 5. In this format, all of the pieces within the block are pieced onto one foundation. Variations of these patterns are sometimes made with other foundation shapes, such as diamonds and hexagons. We define all of these as blocks, since a recognizable unit is complete within the shape (Figure 2-1)

A quilt using any of these patterns could conceivably be, and have been, pieced entirely of one huge "block." However, to make a quilt of

Figure 2-1. Block format: antique Log Cabin blocks.

more than one unit, it is necessary to complete a number of blocks and join them, using the traditional seam-to-seam piecing.

Segment

A segment is a partial unit of a block which cannot be pieced completely on a foundation in block form due to the geometric limitations of the pattern (Figure 2-2). Segments are joined into a block with seam-to-seam piecing (see Chapters 3, 6, 8, and 9). This is a new approach to foundation piecing, combining elements of the block and the piece formats. It opens patterns to foundation piecing that formerly were considered impossible.

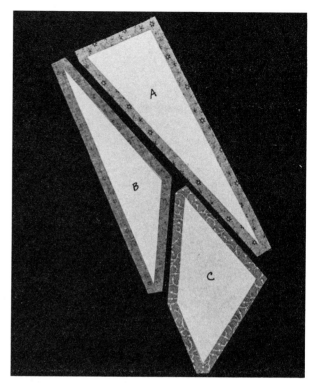

Figure 2-3. Individual foundations.

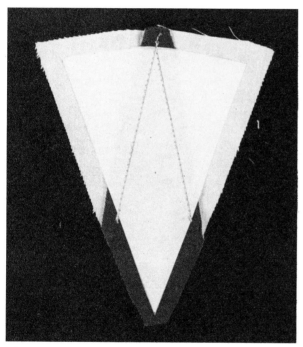

Figure 2-2. Press-pieced segment.

Piece

In contrast to the block or segment, the piece format has an individual foundation for each piece of fabric in the pattern (Figure 2-3). This can provide precision as well as efficient piecing (see Chapters 3, 6, and 7). Pieces are aligned and joined based on the template edge. The resulting precision has great appeal. While the most familiar pattern made with this technique is the hexagon Mosaic, any shape can be used.

Materials

Foundations can be temporary or permanent. In the past, foundations used in pieced quilts were often what was readily available: utility fabric or scraps, or paper of various kinds, such as newspapers, old letters and post cards. Even though the papers could be removed, occasionally they were left in for warmth as well as stability. Today we have more variety available, and can choose foundations that fit our specific requirements.

Permanent Foundations

There are several reasons to leave a foundation in place permanently. Some designs, such as pleated Pineapples, do not lend themselves to quilting and must be pieced on a permanent foundation for stability. On small blocks or quilts using fragile fabric, a foundation can be difficult to remove; removal may, in fact, distort the piecing. On a machine quilted wall hanging, a permanent foundation may add body which will make the piece hang better. A permanent foundation does add the weight of an extra layer; you should consider whether or not this is desirable.

Utility fabric

Lightweight muslin, gingham, batiste, and used fabric make good foundations. An advantage to using fabric is that it can be pieced upon either by hand or machine. It is important that foundation fabric be pre-shrunk before using. It is relatively easy to mark a piecing design on fabric, with several marking options.

Non-woven interfacing

Non-woven interfacing has a firm finish which makes pressed-piecing easy to sew and press open. When used in a piece not requiring batting, such as placemats and table runners, it gives the desirable body and flat appearance. There are many brands of non-woven interfacing of various weights (Sew-Shape, Armo, and Pellon). Choose a weight compatible with your project. Do not use the bias type of interfacing, as it will negate the advantages of a stable foundation. Interfacing foundations can be pieced on either by hand or machine, although they do not needle quite as easily as woven fabric for handsewing. It is used to best advantage when the item will be machine quilted. It is easily marked without distortion, even with a pencil.

Flannel

Flannel can be used as both a foundation and a filler, which makes it possible to hand-quilt without the addition of the extra layer a permanent foundation usually adds. Its use results in a flat look like that of many old quilts, but will not give the "quilty" look of fleece or batting. It is difficult to mark with a pencil, but can be marked with a hot-iron transfer or used in designs when no marking is needed.

Fleece or batting

Fleece or batting can be used as a foundation either alone or with a sub-foundation of fabric or interfacing. Fleece lies flatter and is easier to press on during the piecing process. Batting adds more loft, but distortion in the piecing process is a problem without a sub-foundation. This type of foundation has been used to quilt while piecing, a technique that we feel usually adds speed at the cost of accuracy. Both batting and fleece are difficult to mark with fine lines.

Temporary Foundations

Quilters use temporary foundations primarily when they want to do extensive quilting and don't want the impediment of an extra layer of fabric in the quilt. The temporary foundations we list have the added advantage of firmness. They maintain their shape through the sewing and pressing processes. The only permanent foundation with this property is non-woven interfacing.

We usually leave temporary foundations in place until the blocks are joined, to make it easier to align the blocks. However, on a large quilt the foundations on the inner blocks can be removed after the surrounding blocks are added, to reduce the bulk and weight of the quilt top. We suggest creasing or scoring the foundation along the stitching lines with a blunt implement for easiest removal. This lessens the possibility of stitch damage or fabric distortion.

Experiment with your machine and your fabric to determine the best needle size and stitch length. We get good results with a size 70 or 80 needle and 12–16 stitches to the inch, depending on the fabric. Lynn Graves, who also sews on paper extensively, likes to use a size 90 needle and 20 stitches to the inch which makes it easy to remove the foundation. There is no question that removing foundations is "idiot work" and somewhat messy, but the results are worth it.

Paper

Letter-weight paper, such as typing, computer, or copier paper is inexpensive and readily available. The weight of the paper requires smaller than usual machine stitches to avoid stitch distortion when the paper is removed. This in turn, makes it difficult to correct mistakes. Paper is easily marked and removed after machine stitching. Unfortunately, it sometimes tears out prematurely along the stitching lines.

Tracing paper

Tracing paper has all the advantages of letter-weight paper. An additional advantage is that its lighter weight does not distort the stitch tension as easily when it is removed. It is easy to see through, which can be a definite help when doing some of the more intricate pressed-piecing from the underside. It is easily marked with a variety of methods. There are several grades of tracing paper ranging from an inexpensive lightweight to a heavier rag-based paper. Art and office supply stores carry the largest variety.

Freezer paper

Freezer paper is a relative newcomer as a foundation material and is quickly gaining in popularity. It is available in grocery stores and some quilt shops. It has a dull side which is easily marked, and a shiny side, which will adhere to fabric when pressed with a dry iron. Used for piecing with individual foundations, it usually eliminates basting. It can be easily removed and even re-used a few times. It is useful for pressed-piecing when sewing difficult-to-handle fabric or complicated patterns. Removal may be somewhat more difficult when the seams of the piecing are repeatedly pressed or when steam is used in the iron or if fabric tends to ravel.

All papers, including freezer paper, are available in graphed forms, which can aid in drafting, tracing and stitching. In addition, gridded freezer paper ironed directly onto the fabric can keep the grainline in the pattern pieces consistent. Paper foundations work best for machine stitching. They can be used for hand-piecing only with difficulty because of their stiffness.

Removable interfacing

Removable interfacing has more body than paper. It does not tear until it is deliberately removed. A small stitch is needed to avoid distortion when removing the interfacing. However, stitches are easy to take out when correcting mistakes. It is possible to hand piece on interfacing, but care is needed to avoid breaking the stitches when removing the foundation. Interfacing is more expensive than paper, which is a consideration when making a large quilt. It is easy to mark with a pencil or a hot-iron transfer. We have used Pellon Stitch-N-Tear with success.

Marking Methods

In addition to providing stability, foundation-based piecing gained in popularity when it became apparent that marks could be put onto the foundation which would help assure accuracy in the piecing. These marks ranged from simple guidelines, such as a line or an "x" to a complete replication of the pattern. String and crazy piecing usually did not require extensive marking. The choice of marking techniques is as varied as the choice of foundations. They may, in some cases, be determined by each other (Figure 2-4). Whatever marking method you choose, accuracy is essential.

Figure 2-4. Marking tools.

Basting

Simple marking has been done with a line of basting thread. This can delineate a starting point, boundary lines or pattern lines.

Pencils and pens

Any foundation except batting can be marked with a pencil. Be sure your pencil is kept sharp; a mechanical pencil is ideal. Colored pencils may be helpful. It is important to work slowly and accurately. When marking fabric, use a textured surface such as fine sandpaper or a cutting mat to help prevent the pencil from dragging and stretching the fabric. Check each marked block with your pattern to be sure you have traced accurately.

In some instances a pen can be a good choice for marking a foundation. Care must be taken that the color does not bleed onto the patchwork and that the line drawn is fine enough so that the pattern is true.

Needle punching

Needle punching is an old method of copying patterns, which is applicable to marking paper of almost any weight for foundation use. Pin the pattern to be copied on top of a stack of several layers of paper. With an unthreaded sewing machine, begin at the middle of your pattern and carefully stitch through all layers on the lines. (Figure 2-5). The pattern will be replicated exactly. As an added benefit, the punched holes will keep the stack together.

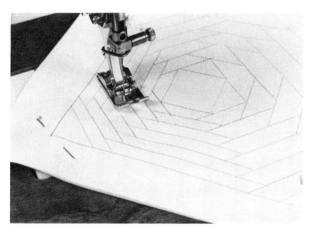

Figure 2-5. Needle punching.

Tracing wheel

Any foundation except batting can be marked with a tracing wheel, using the wheel alone or with the colored carbon paper used for marking fabric.

Hot-iron transfer

This method offers faster marking, since a transfer can be used many times before renewing the marking. Once the transfer has been checked for accuracy, you are guaranteed repeatable blocks. This method works well with fabric and interfacing foundations.

Pencils for making a hot-iron transfer are available at craft, sewing, quilt, and variety stores. Follow the specific directions which come with the pencil for making a transfer. The pencils are used to trace the pattern onto paper. This paper becomes the "transfer" which is then pressed onto the foundation with a hot dry iron. Use a good quality tracing paper such as rag paper to make your transfer so that it will not be burned by the iron.

Copy machine

Patterns can be reproduced and pieced on copier paper. Be sure to check a copy with your

original pattern to be sure it has not been distorted in one or both directions by the machine. When making repeat copies, always work from the original; copies of copies increase the possibility of distortion. It is possible to use a freshly-made copy as a hot-iron transfer. The lines will be light.

Pre-marked blocks

Several types of pre-marked blocks, both paper and fabric, are commercially available. See Resources for a list of some of them. These offer convenience and accuracy at a reasonable price if you can find the pattern in the size you need.

Stamps

There are stamps available for marking foundations that will mark on paper or fabric. Your local office supply store may be able to have a custom stamp made for you, but the price may make it prohibitive unless you plan to use it a great deal.

Stencils

Patterns can be marked on foundations using pre-cut stencils which you can either purchase or make yourself. Care must be taken in marking the foundations to avoid distorting the pattern.

Piecing Techniques

For foundation work in general, and for the specific projects in the book, you will need basic sewing supplies to include needles, pins, scissors, glue stick, clear plastic ruler, sharp pencil, graph paper, colored pencils. A rotary cutter and mat are desirable. Some patterns require templates made to mark the foundations or fabric accurately. The best material we have found is an opaque lightweight plastic that can be cut with scissors, with a matt finish so that it can be drawn on easily.

Piecing to most quiltmakers means sewing two pieces of fabric together, seam-to-seam (Figure 2-6). Foundation piecing to most usually means pressed-piecing or English template piecing. Actually, foundation-based piecing can involve all of these techniques.

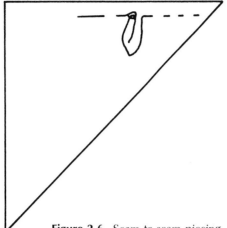

Figure 2-6. Seam-to-seam piecing.

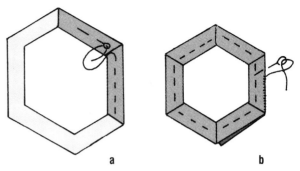

Figure 2-7a. English template piecing, basting fabric to template. b. English template piecing, shapes being joined.

Our projects were largely made with a sewing machine. We prefer this method of construction because of the strength and speed of machine stitching on all types of foundations.

Hand sewing, if desired, can be used with most foundation formats. We often hand-stitch short or set-in seams such as those in the *High Rise* quilt in Chapter 7. With pressed-piecing, hand sewing is easier with permanent foundation materials such as fabric.

Single Foundation Piecing

Single foundation piecing is a non-pressed-piecing technique using individual foundations the finished size of the pieces to be joined. The foundations are attached to the fabric patches. When the edges of the patches are matched and the pieces are stitched together, the resulting pieced work is precise and sharp.

English template piecing is an example from the past, still done today. An individual foundation, of heavy paper, is cut for each piece in the quilt. The seam allowance is basted over the foundation, providing an exact shape of the finished size (Figure 2-7a). The shapes are aligned, right sides facing, and the edges are whipped together (Figure 2-7b). While a variety of patterns have been done with this technique, the most familiar to us is the hexagon Mosaic.

A more contemporary use of single template piecing uses freezer paper foundations. Each is ironed onto fabric with a dry iron. The pieces are then joined in seam-to-seam stitching, using the foundations as guides (Figure 2-8). This provides

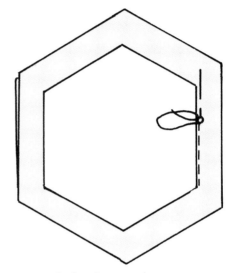

Figure 2-8. Single foundation with seam-to-seam piecing.

an accurate stitching line, especially useful for small or irregular shapes. It avoids the tedious basting and whip-stitching of English template piecing while retaining the precision.

Pressed Piecing

Most foundation blocks are constructed using pressed-piecing techniques. Pressed piecing is done by laying a piece of fabric on the foundation, wrong side against the foundation. This piece is not stitched down. The next piece is placed on top of the first, right sides together, with the edges aligned and stitched through all layers. The second fabric is opened to the right side and pressed. Depending on the pattern, the fabric may be cut or trimmed before the next piece is added. Subsequent pieces of fabric are added by repeating the process, following the pattern.

There are two approaches to this technique that are largely interchangeable. One is done with the fabric on *top* of the foundation, using fabric-placement lines. The second is done with the fabric *under* the foundaton, using sewing lines marked on the top of the foundation. Properly done, blocks made by both techniques can be joined with precision.

The choice of which pressed-piecing technique to use is dictated by the pattern, by the foundation, or by personal preference. *Top* pressed-piecing is probably more appealing to those comfortable with machine piecing and who sew with a consistent seam allowance. *Under* pressed-piecing is often chosen by those who prefer sewing on an exact line, whether by hand or machine. Most patterns can be done by either technique, but some are more workable with one or the other. Miniatures, for instance, are easier and more precise constructed with *under* piecing.

The following directions, using a basic Log Cabin block as an example, will clarify the two methods. Log Cabin blocks are traditionally pieced with light and dark fabric. In this pattern, numbers indicate the piecing order. You will alternate using light twice (on the odd numbers) and dark twice (on the even numbers) throughout the block (Figure 2-9).

The firmness of the foundation may at first

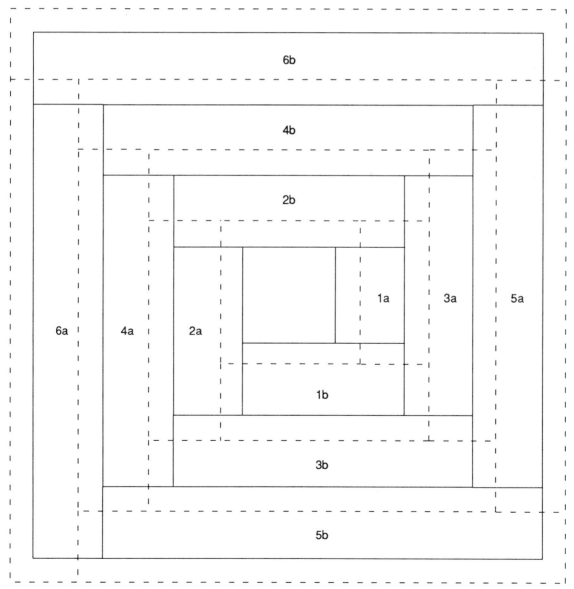

Figure 2-9. Log Cabin pattern with piecing order marked. Dotted lines are fabric placement lines for top piecing. Solid lines are sewing lines for under piecing.

seem awkward to work with because of the unaccustomed bulk or stiffness. A good strategy for handling any foundation as you are piecing is to roll it to the area being pieced. This avoids crumpling and prematurely tearing the foundation (Figure 2-10).

Figure 2-10. Rolling a foundation for easy handling.

Top Pressed-Piecing

All *top* piecing foundations, except those for Crazy and random String blocks, are marked with fabric placement lines. This is the line on which the cut edge of the fabric is laid. The finished edge of the fabric will be $\frac{1}{4}''$ (or the width of your presser foot) from the marked line. A consistent seam allowance is essential for precision. It is possible to prepare any pattern for *top* pressed-piecing by adding fabric placement lines to every line in the pattern.

Cut one strip each of light and dark fabric $1\frac{1}{4}''$ wide, and a scant $1\frac{1}{2}''$ square of a contrasting color. This includes a $\frac{1}{4}''$ seam allowance. If the distance from the edge of your presser foot to the needle on your machine differs from $\frac{1}{4}''$, either adjust the needle of your machine to fit the seam allowance, adjust the seam allowance to fit your measurement or purchase a new presser foot. It is necessary to have accurate control of the seam allowance in one of these ways because the seam guides on the throat plate of your machine will be covered by the foundation.

Trace the dotted lines from the pattern onto a foundation (Figure 2-9).

Attach the square to the center of the block along the drawn lines, with a pin or glue stick. Be sure the lines around the square can be seen (Figure 2-11).

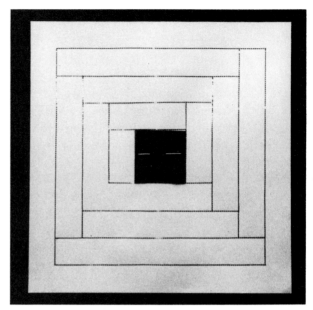

Figure 2-11. Center square pinned in place.

Lay a light strip along one edge of the square, right side down. The cut edges of the fabric should be aligned with the drawn line. It is not necessary to pin the top strip. Keeping the edge of your presser foot along the drawn line, stitch with a $\frac{1}{4}$ inch seam allowance (Figure 2-12).

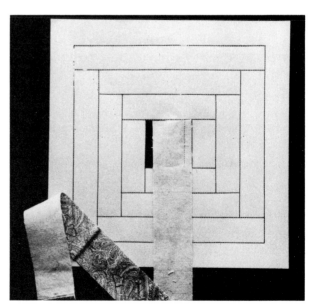

Figure 2-12. First strip sewn.

Open the strip and press. The edge of the strip should be aligned with the next fabric-placement line (Figure 2-13). If it is not, or if it extends over the line, correct this seam allowance as explained above. Re-stitch if necessary.

Figure 2-13. First strip opened and pressed.

Cut the strip. To cut quickly and accurately, lay your scissors on the fabric with the blade open. Pull the fabric across the lower blade. Slide the scissors to the next line and cut (Figure 2-14). Pin the strip to the foundation, again taking care that the fabric does not cover the drawn line. Add another strip of the same color (Figure 2-15).

Figure 2-14. Cutting technique.

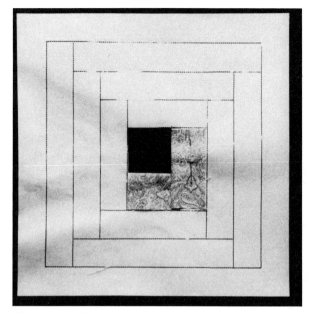

Figure 2-15. First color progression completed.

Continue piecing around the block, following the piecing order and giving the block a quarter turn each time. Change colors as indicated, every two logs (Figure 2-16). Take care that the fabric does not cover the line. This is important, since the line is your guide for a proper seam allowance. When the block is complete, turn it over and trim off any fabric extending over the edge of the foundation (Figure 2-17).

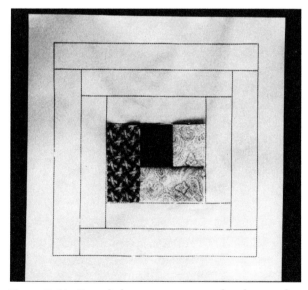

Figure 2-16. First dark strip sewn, opened and pressed.

Figure 2-17. Completed Log Cabin block.

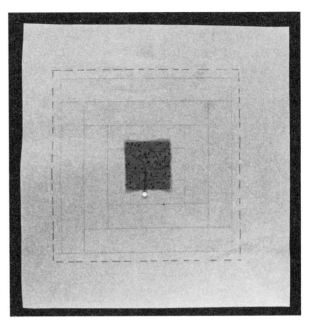

Figure 2-18. Center square pinned onto under side of foundation.

Under Pressed-Piecing

All *under* piecing foundations are marked with a sewing line. This is indicated on the Log Cabin pattern by the solid lines. Seam allowance must be added to these measurements.

Cut one strip each, light and dark fabric 1¼″ wide, and a generous 1½″ square of contrasting color fabric for the center. This includes a ¼″ seam allowance.

Trace the solid lines and the final outside dotted line from the Log Cabin pattern (Figure 2-9) onto a foundation. A transparent foundation like tracing paper is a good choice for this technique.

Be aware that with *under* pressed-piecing, the drawn pattern is reversed and will result in a mirror image. This is only a problem if the direction of your pattern is important. If it is, a simple way to maintain the original design is to invert the pattern when tracing it. Other methods of avoiding a mirror image when tracing a pattern for under piecing are listed in the Index.

Attach the fabric square to the center of the foundation, on the under or undrawn side, with a pin or glue stick. It should cover the lines of the center square with an adequate ¼″ seam allowance on all sides (Figure 2-18). If you are not using a transparent foundation, it may be necessary to stab pins through the lines from the top side in order to center the square properly.

Cut a piece of light fabric the length of one side of the square. Place it on the square, right sides together, with the cut edges matching. Pin the strip, placing the pin away from the sewing line (Figure 2-19).

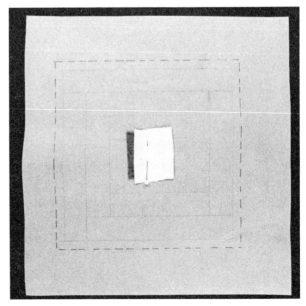

Figure 2-19. First strip pinned in place.

Turn the foundation over so that the fabric is against the feed dogs and the lines are visible on the top. Make sure the pin is out of the way. Stitch on the marked line (Figure 2-20). After

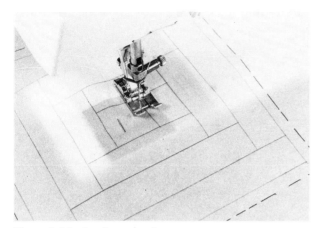

Figure 2-20. Stitching the first strip.

sewing, turn the foundation back over and trim the seams to a scant $\frac{1}{4}''$ (Figure 2-21). Open the pieces, press in place and pin (Figure 2-22).

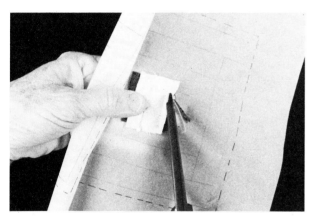

Figure 2-21. Trimming the seam allowance.

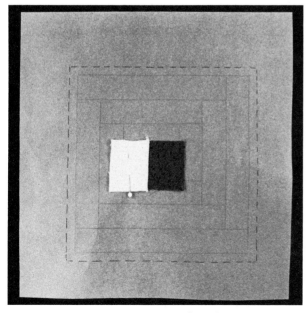

Figure 2-22. First light strip pinned in place.

Give the block a quarter-turn. Use the side of the center square plus the end of the strip already sewn onto it as a measure, and cut another piece of the light strip (Figure 2-23). Lay that strip on, right sides facing, with the cut edges matching. Turn the block over, as before, with the fabric next to the feed dogs, and stitch on the drawn line. Open the piece, press and pin (Figure 2-24).

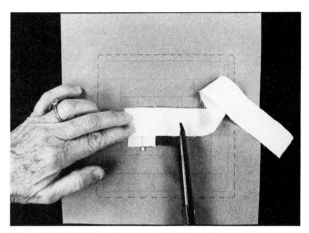

Figure 2-23. Measuring second light strip.

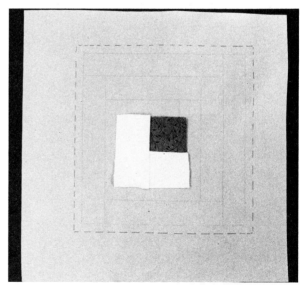

Figure 2-24. First color progression completed.

Continue piecing around the block, turning it one quarter each time, sewing on the marked side of the foundation. Alternate two light strips with two dark strips (Figure 2-25). Be sure to trim excess seam allowance as you go, since it will become trapped by subsequent seams.

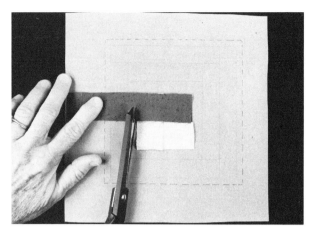

Figure 2-25. Measuring first dark strip.

The cut edge of the outer strips will cover the final dotted line. The solid line will be the guide for joining the block to another block. After stitching and pressing the last strips, stay-stitch the block on the outer dotted line and trim all the excess fabric to that line (Figures 2-26 and 2-27).

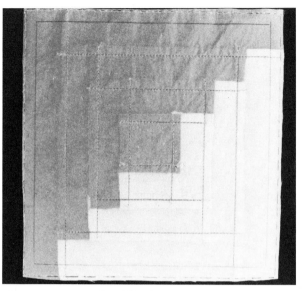

Figure 2-26. Completed block from foundation side.

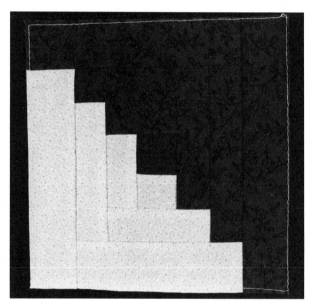

Figure 2-27. Completed block. Note mirror image from Figure 2-26.

Plate 1. Antique *String Star*. Maker unknown, circa 1890. 94″ × 98″. From the collection of Kathlyn F. Sullivan, Raleigh, N.C.

Plate 2. *Garden Party.* Caryl Bryer Fallert, Oswego, Ill., 1989. 49″ × 61″. Photo courtesy of the artist.

Plate 3. *San Andreas.* Barbara Elwell, Raleigh, N.C., 1989. 22″ × 36″. From the collection of Sarah Stang, Washington, D.C.

Plate 4. *Scintilla.* Jane Hall, 1990. 35″ × 35″.

Plate 5. *Opus One.* Sonja Shogren, Raleigh, N.C., 1991. 18″ × 18″.

Plate 6. *Ramblers.* Mary Golden, New Hampton, N.H., 1990. 84″ × 84″. From the collection of Kathy Schiell, Schroon Lake, N.Y.

Plate 7. Victorian Crazy Quilt. Maker unknown, circa 1880. 68″ × 68″. From the collection of Dixie Haywood.

Plate 8. Victorian Crazy Quilt. Maker unknown, circa 1890. 39″ × 72″. From the collection of Julia Wernicke, Pensacola, Florida.

Plate 9. *Chromania.* Dixie Haywood, 1990. 90″ × 90″.

Plate 10. *Redcubes.* Dixie Haywood, 1985. 69″ × 84″.

Plate 11. *Dawn's Early Light.* Dixie Haywood, 1990. 73″ × 80″.
From the collection of Lands' End, Inc.

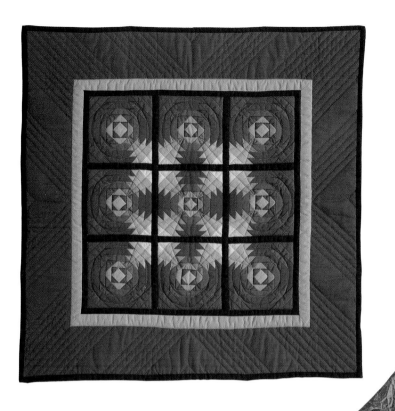

Plate 12. *Ora pro Nobis.* Dixie Haywood, 1990. 20″ × 20″.

Plate 13. *Iridescent Ripples.* Jane Hall, 1989. 15″ × 15″. From the collection of Sue Hall, Raleigh, N.C.

Plate 14. *Tori Forest.* Jane Hall, 1990. 31″ x 31″.

Plate 15. *The Good Earth.* Janet Elwin, Damariscotta, Maine, 1983. 102″ × 110″.

Plate 16. *Refraction #4–7.* Caryl Bryer Fallert, Oswego, Ill., 1990. 88″ × 92″. Photo by Jerry DeFelice.

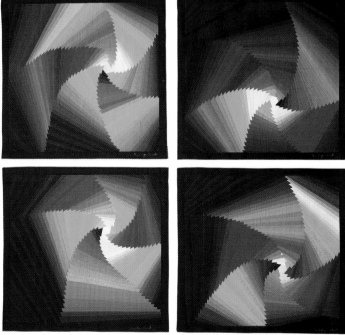

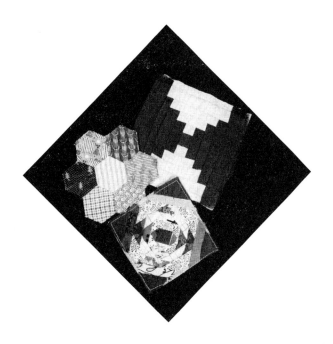

Introduction to Design Categories

The following chapters explore design categories that either traditionally have been pieced on a foundation, or for which we and other contemporary quilters have devised foundation techniques.

Each chapter will survey the background and design of a category and its contemporary application to foundation piecing. We discuss blocks, and include patterns for some, to give you a quick visualization of the concepts. "Getting Started" projects in each chapter will give you a mini-lesson so that you can try foundations with the techniques inherent in the design. It is our hope that the projects will introduce you to the advantages of foundation-based piecing with both favorite patterns and designs that you have always wanted to try.

As you read—and hopefully try—the Getting Started projects, notice the different ways that foundations are used by the contributors. Notice the variations in techniques using the same foundations. Notice also the combinations of piecing techniques possible. There are many ways of using foundations to achieve accuracy, stability, and innovation; that's what this book is all about.

Those interested in studying a design category more extensively will find resources listed in the Bibliography at the end of the book.

CHAPTER 3

String Piecing

String patterns essentially create fabric from a variety of smaller pieces, whether true scraps or selected yardage. Most often in the past these were strips of varying widths, even selvedges, all of which were referred to as "strings." The fabric is press-pieced onto a foundation, in either a random or controlled fashion. Early string quilts tended to be crude and utilitarian.

Covering a foundation square with diagonal or, less commonly, horizontal strings is among the simplest forms of this pattern (Figure 3-1). As blocks are rotated and joined, different patterns are formed by the juxtaposition of the strings (Figure 3-2). It is also possible to create a larger piece of "fabric" from which multiple blocks or segments can be cut. The size and color of the strips sewn onto the foundation can be random, giving a charming scrap look to the pattern, as in the antique String Star quilt in Color Plate 1. The construction of this quilt is unusual because the stars are machine appliquéd to the background

Figure 3-1. Detail of Figure 3-2, diagonally pieced string top, with fragments of the foundations still in place.

rather than being pieced in. When the size and colors of the strips are planned, the design is more unified and controlled.

Increased familiarity with the technique led quilters to explore the design possibilities. They

Figure 3-2. Diagonally pieced string top, showing rotated patterns. From the collection of Barbara Elwell, Raleigh, N.C.

experimented with color placement and created graphic designs with their scraps. They used hard-to-handle fabrics such as silks and velvets as well as the more prosaic cottons (Figure 3-3).

Foundations in shapes other than squares were used to extend fabrics and create designs.

Figure 3-3. Antique string quilt top, horizontally pieced, of silks and velvets.

Most common were the diamonds used for four, six, or eight-pointed stars (Figure 3-4). The small quilt on the chapter opener is a contemporary four-pointed string star made by Gladys Baker, Zebulon, N.C. Another common shape was the triangle, used to form a Spider Web and other patterns. The strips were often laid on these foundations horizontally, which created secondary designs when the pieced segments were put together (Figure 3-5).

Figure 3-4. Antique string star block.

Figure 3-5. Spiderweb pattern construction.

Utility fabrics as well as newspapers seem to have been the primary foundation materials used in the past for string piecing. When the newspapers have been left in, it sometimes is possible to date the piece by reading the scraps of paper (Figure 3-6). Random strings are most often press-pieced on *top* of the foundation without marked lines. When it is important to match color, *under* pressed-piecing can be advantageous. When using segments of a block such as in our "Getting Started" project, you will need either single foundation piecing or seam-to-seam piecing to complete the block.

Figure 3-6. Newspaper foundations, circa 1939.

Contemporary quilters have carried this technique far beyond its homely origins. Caryl Bryer Fallert has taken string piecing to new and exciting heights. She uses string piecing as a design element, creating movement, mood and rhythm with her piecing and her exceptional use of color. To make *Garden Party* (Color Plate 2), Caryl cut apart a full-size paper drawing. She used all the techniques for foundation work in this one quilt. Each section of her drawing was used as a foundation, either as a base for *top* or *under* pressed-piecing or for single foundation piecing. The single foundations were attached to the fabric pieces with a glue stick.

To complete the quilt top, these segments were then joined, using seam-to-seam piecing and a technique Caryl has developed. She calls this hybrid between piecing and appliqué "En-glish Machine Piecing," and uses it in areas that have many curves and tight points. To join two pieces, she presses the edge of one piece over its foundation, and positions it on top of the other at the sewing line, right sides together. She joins them with a narrow machine zigzag stitch using invisible thread, extending the zigzag stitch only a thread or two into the folded edge. This gives her the absolute accuracy of English template piecing with the speed of the sewing machine.

Barbara Elwell made yardage of strips and strings from the ends of bolts of fabric, by press-piecing them onto muslin. She cut pinwheel shapes to make *Primer* (Figure 3-7). These shapes give a focus to the random-string piecing.

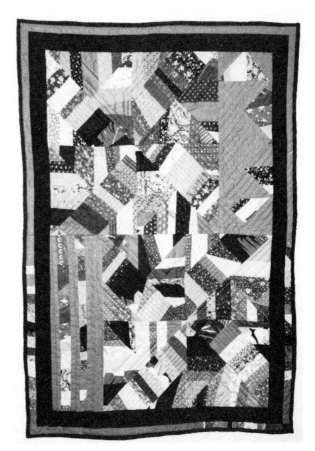

Figure 3-7. *Primer* wall quilt, Barbara Elwell, Raleigh, N.C.

Barbara pieces on foundations to use scraps of silk and Thai ikat cotton leftover from making clothes. She saves anything wider than one-half inch; random-string piecing allows her to use the entire scrap. With experience she has learned to control her designs by deliberate placement of color values, creating rich and subtle patterns such as *San Andreas* (Color Plate 3). The foundations also help her control these fabrics which vary widely in weave and weight, and ravel easily. Barbara's innovative work is a prime example of how the most basic form of this traditional design continues to be timeless.

Jane's quilt, *Scintilla* (Color Plate 4) is an Op Art construction. This genre of designs is composed of controlled sets of strips which intersect with strips of the opposite color value. This creates illusions of depth and dimension as well as circular motion without the use of curved lines.

■ Getting Started ■

Illusions Block
(Figure 3-8)

Figure 3-8. Illusions block.

This is a simple Op Art design. Piecing this block, with sharp color contrast to give the three-dimensional illusion, requires absolute accuracy at the points where the horizontal and vertical planes intersect. Creating fabric by *under* pressed-piecing onto freezer paper gives the control and precision needed to do this.

1. To draft the pattern, draw a 12″ square with a square on point in the center, measuring 3″ from point to point (Figure 3-9a). Extend the lines from the square to each corner (Figure 3-9b). Draw lines $\frac{3}{4}$″ apart in the triangles formed (Figure 3-9c). Connect the triangle lines across the diagonal columns (Figure 3-9d). This pattern gives the finished measurements of the block.

2. To make the large triangular units for one block, draw eight horizontal lines measured as shown in Figure 3-10 on the dull side of a rectangle of freezer paper measuring at least 7″ × 28″. Position the freezer paper panel over your drafted block so that the long side of the triangle is $\frac{1}{4}$″ inside the outer drawn line of the chart, and trace the triangle onto the panel. This allows a $\frac{1}{4}$″ seam allowance on the long edge. Repeat this process, nesting the four triangles along the panel, leaving space for adequate seam allowances between them (Figure 3-10)

3. Choose two fabrics with sharply contrasting colors, such as the red and white in our example. Busy prints are not as effective with this type of design as solids or prints that read as solids. Cut strips $1\frac{1}{2}$″ wide by 28″ long, four from the red and three from the white fabric. This is a slightly larger width than is necessary and it will need to be trimmed after stitching to leave $\frac{1}{4}$″ seam allowance.

4. Lay a red strip, right side up, along one edge of the shiny side of the freezer paper at the outer drawn line. The other edge of this strip will

Figure 3-9a. Drafting Illusions: center square in place. *b*. Lines of square extended diagonally to corners of block. *c*. Horizontal and vertical lines drawn in. *d*. Diagonal cross lines connected.

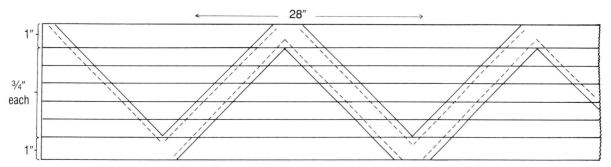

Figure 3-10. Chart for triangular unit strip panel.

overlap the next drawn line by $\frac{1}{4}''$. Position the strip by pre-pressing at intervals along its length with the tip of the iron, before pressing it into place. Align a white strip with the red, right sides together, and pin. Turn the freezer paper to the dull side and stitch on the drawn line. Trim seams to a scant $\frac{1}{4}''$ as you go, to avoid shadowing-through of the darker fabric. Open the strip and press it onto the freezer paper. To be sure the strips are even and flat, turn the freezer paper over and press also from the underside. Take care not to iron the uncovered areas of the paper.

Repeat across the foundation, alternating colors. Add $\frac{1}{4}''$ seam allowances to the drawn lines of the triangles and cut on the dotted lines as indicated in Figure 3-10. The seam allowance at the bottom of each triangle is built in. Since the top of the triangle is a white strip, it will be necessary to pick out a few stitches and remove the remnant of the red fabric at the very top of each triangle.

5. To make the diagonal strips, cut a piece of freezer paper at least 6″ × 20″ and mark it according to Figure 3-11. As with the triangle strip, this chart includes both the piecing lines and the outlines of the finished shapes. It is most accurate to simply trace the lines for these panels from your draft. Leave a 1″ space between the panels. Cut strips as follows: From red fabric, two strips 2″ × 6″; six strips $1\frac{3}{4}''$ × 6″. From white fabric, one strip $2\frac{3}{4}''$ × 6″; six strips $1\frac{3}{4}''$ × 6″. *Under* press-piece as before, beginning with the $2\frac{3}{4}''$ strip in the center of the panel. Add $\frac{1}{4}''$ seam allowance to the shapes, as indicated by the dotted lines on the chart (Figure 3-11) and cut out

the panels. This will result in one long strip and two short ones; remove the excess piece of white fabric between the short strips.

6. To assemble the block, stab pins through the lines matching the seams of the strips and the triangles exactly, at the color change lines. The paper will hold the fabric firmly, and the joins will match. Press the seams open so that the bulk in the seams will not roll the points out of alignment.

7. To retain the design when joining multiple blocks of this pattern, it is necessary to separate the blocks with a strip of the light fabric. Adding a border of light fabric to a single block gives it greater depth. Remove the freezer paper once the block is bordered.

Party Time
by Jane Hall and Dixie Haywood
(Color Plate 27)

Elegant fabrics were more often used for Crazy Quilts and Mosaic patchwork than for string piecing. Our project, *Party Time*, uses silks and satins and *top* pressed-piecing to make a string star (Figure 3-12). We used freezer paper as a foundation since the slippery difficult-to-use fabrics would adhere to the paper when pressed, giving us stability and control. We used two methods of string piecing to illustrate the different options available.

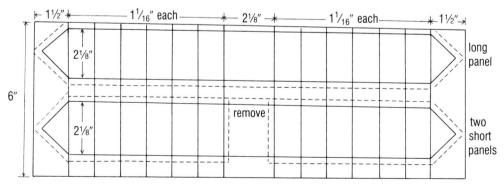

Figure 3-11. Chart for diagonal unit strip panels.

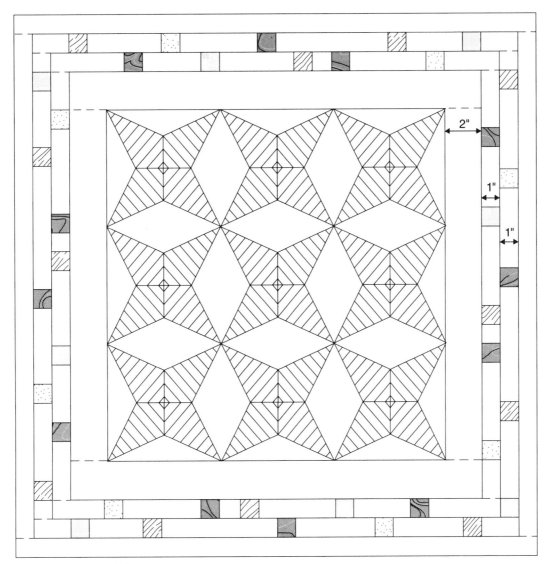

Figure 3-12. *Party Time* quilt layout.

The string pieced points of the stars are segments which then must be completed using either single foundation piecing (see Chapter 2) or ordinary seam-to-seam piecing. Because of the scale of the piecing as well as the tendency to fray of the fabrics we selected, we left the freezer paper in the stars as permanent foundations.

Quilt Size: 28″ × 28″

Block Size: 6″ (nine blocks)

Materials

Six to eight silk and satin fabrics cut into approximately 45 strips, 18″ long and varying from ¾ inch to one inch wide

One yard navy cotton for background and borders

Backing, batting, binding

Freezer paper; template plastic

Construction Directions

1. Make plastic templates from A (star point), B (background diamond) and C (background half-diamond). Do not add seam allowances (Figure 3-13).

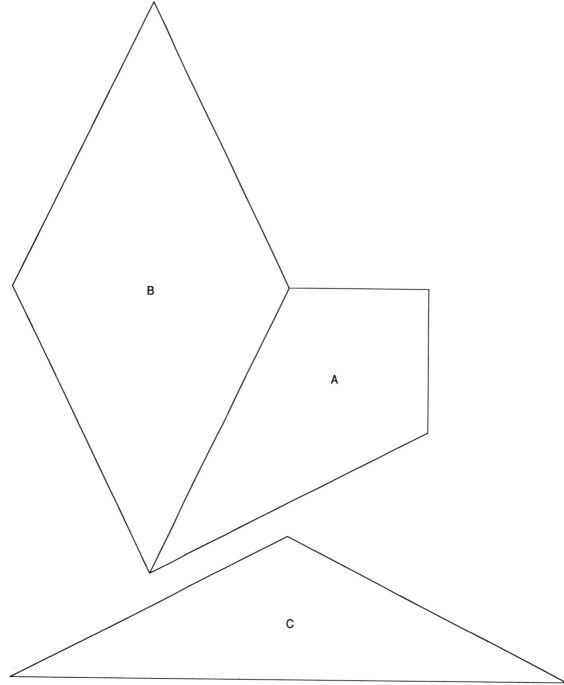

Figure 3-13. Templates for *Party Time*.

2. Cut the following from freezer paper: 4 strips 5″ × 18″; Template A, 4 pieces; Templates B and C, 12 pieces each.

3. Using the first string piecing method, creating fabric, choose 9 or 10 color strips of random widths. Determine the color progression you wish and press the first strip right side up, along an edge on the shiny side of a 5″ × 18″ foundation.

4. Using *top* pressed-piecing, stitch the next color in place. Open the strip and press it to the foundation, taking care that you press the fabric rather than the uncovered freezer paper. Press evenly so that there are no bulges or pleats in the

"straight" strip. If you want the fabric narrower, trim the strip before adhering the fabric to the foundation. Repeat the process until the foundation is covered with fabric.

5. On the foundation side of this panel, draw around Template A. Add a seam allowance, cutting ¼" from the drawn line with a rotary cutter. Nest the shapes across the foundation and cut 7 more (Figure 3-14).

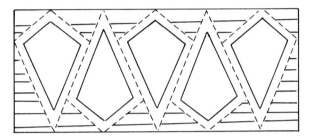

Figure 3-14. Layout for cutting star points.

6. Press-piece strips of fabric to the remaining 3 large foundations and cut out the star points. They can be matched with the same progression of color, alternated from the same foundation to reverse colors within a star, or completely mixed by using points from different foundations. You will need a total of 32 star point segments.

7. Align the drawn lines of two star point segments and stitch them together on the lines. Do not stitch into the seam allowances. Complete eight stars, each with four segments.

8. For another string piecing technique, piece the remaining star on individual foundations. Press-piece fabric strips onto the four freezer paper foundations cut from Template A in Step 1, being sure that fabric extends at least ¼" beyond the foundation. Trim the excess fabric, leaving a ¼" seam allowance. Join the pieces into a star, using the edge of the foundation as a sewing guide.

9. Press the freezer paper foundations of B and C onto the navy fabric, allowing space for seam allowances between them. Cut out, adding ¼ inch seam allowance on all sides to each piece. Join B and C pieces to stars according to the quilt layout (see Figure 3-12).

When piecing where four stars meet, you may want to carefully remove the foundation from the seam allowances at the points of the stars for easier handling. (Figure 3-15). Sew on the lines, taking care not to extend the stitching into the seam allowance.

Figure 3-15. Reverse of quilt showing panel foundations and individual foundations, with selective removal of foundations for easier piecing.

10. For the interior border, cut two widths of navy fabric, 2½" wide. Stitch in place, sewing first the sides and then the top and bottom.

11. To make the pieced border, cut a width of navy fabric 6" wide. Cut it into pieces using the measurements for the Row 1 and 2 panels in Figure 3-16. Cut ten freezer paper foundations, 1" × 6". Cut ten strips of the colors used in the stars, 1½" × 6". Press the freezer paper to the centers of the colored strips.

Row 1

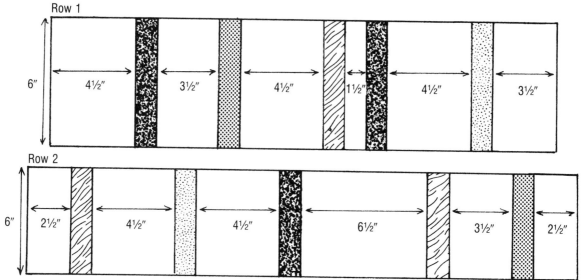

Row 2

Figure 3-16. Piecing charts for borders. Measurements given are cut sizes.

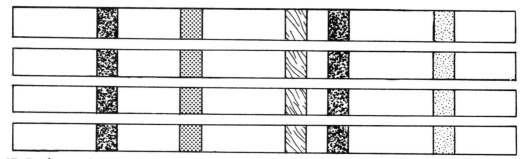

Figure 3-17. Border panel cuts.

12.   Piece each panel, alternating navy and color strips, using the foundations on the colored strips as stitching guides. Cut each section crosswise into four strips, each $1\frac{1}{2}''$ wide (Figure 3-17).

13.   For Row 1, cut 1 inch from each end of two of the strips to make the side borders. On the freezer paper, mark the seam allowances on the foundations of the colors to ensure that the borders including the squares will finish as 1''. Stitch the side borders first, following with the top and bottom, sewing so that the colors rotate clockwise around the quilt. Repeat the process with the Row 2 section. Remove the border foundations.

14.   For the final border, cut two strips of navy fabric, $1\frac{1}{2}'' \times 26\frac{1}{2}''$, and two strips $1\frac{1}{2}'' \times 28\frac{1}{2}''$. Stitch them to the quilt as you did in Step 10.

15.   Baste, quilt, and bind with navy fabric. We used machine quilting "in the ditch" to emphasize the star shapes. The navy background areas were quilted with a curved pattern and the border was quilted in the ditch around the confetti areas.

CHAPTER 4

Crazy Piecing

Crazy piecing, like string piecing, has always been worked on a foundation. It differs from string piecing in that it is composed of fabric in random sizes and shapes rather than with strips alone. The foundation is left unmarked as there is not a specific pattern line that needs to be followed. The crazy quilts made during the Victorian era with fancy fabrics, elaborately embellished, had more elements of appliqué collage than of pressed piecing, although both techniques traditionally have been associated with this design. (Color Plate 7).

The appeal of the crazy quilt did not die with the Victorian era. However, to duplicate the Victorian look, as Julia Wernicke did in *This is Your Life* (Figures 4-1 and 4-2), a quilter needs sophisticated skills in embroidery and other embellishments. In contrast to this contemporary quilt with a Victorian look, Julia's antique Crazy Quilt (Color Plate 8) transcends its Victorian origin

Figure 4-1. *This is Your Life* by Julia Wernicke, Pensacola, FL. 1981. 31″ × 42″. Collection of Mr. and Mrs. Michael C. Edlebeck.

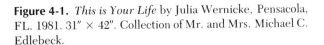

Figure 4-2. Detail showing contemporary motifs.

with a more contemporary linear format as well as elements of string piecing.

Dixie's approach to crazy piecing is to consider it a technique rather than a style. A style is time-based, focusing on a specific era such as that of the embellished Victorian crazy quilt; a technique is open-ended, making it adaptable to any design, traditional to contemporary. Crazy piecing should be seen as a design-in-the-cloth, free-form method of creating fabric that has possibilities for use in both pieced and appliquéd quilts. *Top* pressed-piecing is used with this technique.

Crazy piecing can appear as a diagonally pieced block difficult to distinguish from a ran-

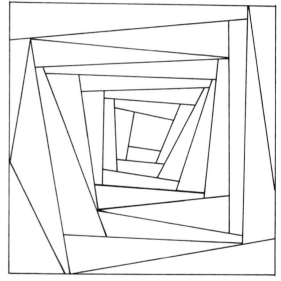

Figure 4-3. Diagonal (top) and Log Cabin configuration blocks.

dom-width string, or as a repetitive symmetrical form reminiscent of a Log Cabin (Figure 4-3). It can also assume the type of free motion seen in *Chromania* (Color Plate 9). It can be pieced on shapes and in segments of a design (Figure 4-4).

Figure 4-4. Star constructed of crazy piecing segments.

Foundations for crazy piecing have generally been fabric, and only a small percentage of the quilts were quilted (Figure 4-5). Victorian crazy quilts, with their emphasis on embellishment, were for show rather than use as bed-

Figure 4-5. Antique wool crazy quilt top.

covers. Utility crazy quilts made from wool were often tied; when made from cotton they were sometimes quilted, with the foundation acting as the filler (Figure 4-6).

Figure 4-6. Machine quilted antique cotton crazy quilt.

This is one of the few design categories that can be pieced over fleece or batting since the only precision needed is that the blocks be the same size. Although piecing on fleece alone can be done with care, use a sub-foundation when piecing on batting to avoid distortion.

Dixie often has pieced on a "blank," consisting of batting stitched to a foundation, especially when the piece did not require hand quilting. She has pieced over batting alone to create additional dimension when the segment was used in a quilt top and hand quilted (Figure 4-7). In recent years her crazy piecing for quilts has been done with removable foundations, allowing quilting to assume more importance in the total design of

Figure 4-7. Crazy quilt diamonds pieced over batting for added dimension.

the quilt. She works on a foundation cut to the size needed, rather than creating fabric from which pieces are cut, so that designs formed by the piecing can be controlled. The result of this can be seen in *Redcubes* (Color Plate 10) and *Chromania* (Color Plate 9).

Both quilts use same-fabric crazy quilting, which adds texture and motion to color blocks that cannot be achieved by quilting alone. Same-fabric crazy quilting is created when an entire block or segment is pieced using only one fabric. Solid fabric used in this way has subtle color variations caused by changes in the grain line; this is especially effective with polished cottons and blends.

The motion achieved in both quilts, often commented upon, is due to several factors. Piecing begins near the center of the foundation and proceeds fairly evenly in all directions. Pressed-pieced crazy quilting creates longer and longer lines as it builds. These are reduced by cuts with two or more edges. By starting in the center, the proportions remain consistent even though the pieces become longer (Figure 4-8).

Figure 4-8. Center-based crazy piecing.

Another element creating motion is the type of cuts made as the piecing proceeds. Triangles, curves and narrow strips add motion; squares and rectangles do not. Color also plays a part. Visual flow and balance is helped by using a color palette that usually includes several shades of from three to five colors.

These obviously are guidelines rather than rules. *Redcubes*, for instance, achieves motion in the crazy pieced blocks with only one fabric in each colored section. *Chromania* uses no curves in the piecing. If it had been desired to have the focus in the center of the quilt, rather than in the four solid-color motifs, it could have been achieved by starting the piecing of the four large triangles in the middle of the quilt at the right angles of the triangles.

Crazy piecing is a process of learning to see and control the emerging graphics as you design in the cloth. The ability to do this improves rapidly with practice. The following small piece is an ideal place to start.

■ Getting Started ■

Chromania Too
by Dixie Haywood
(Color Plate 28)

This project uses crazy piecing to create fabric for a skewed nine-patch on point (Figure 4-9). The nine patches are each same-fabric crazy piecing; the corner triangles are multi-fabric crazy piecing.

Figure 4-9. *Chromania Too* quilt layout.

Tracing paper is used for the foundations. The border uses *under* pressed-piecing and the remainder of the quilt uses *top* pressed-piecing. The segments of the quilt are joined together with seam-to-seam piecing.

Quilt Size: 16″ × 16″

Materials
Solid fabric: small amounts of nine colors, plus grey

Print fabric: small amounts of four or five greys
Backing fabric; batting; navy binding
Tracing paper; template plastic

General Crazy Piecing Directions
To crazy piece, precut a piece of fabric and pin it right side up near the center of the foundation (Figure 4-10)

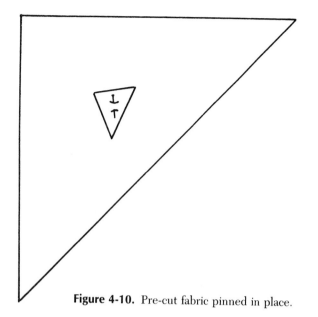

Figure 4-10. Pre-cut fabric pinned in place.

Lay an uncut piece of fabric right side down along one edge of the first piece and stitch through all layers with a $\frac{1}{4}''$ seam allowance. Do not pin the upper fabric, and do not stitch beyond the under fabric (Figure 4-11).

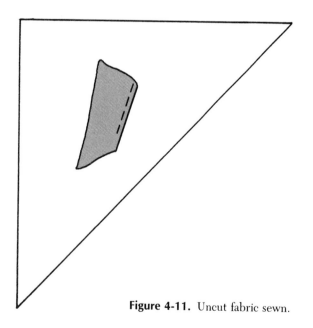

Figure 4-11. Uncut fabric sewn.

Open the fabric, press, and cut to the shape desired (Figure 4-12). Pin the cut piece to the

foundation (Figure 4-13). Once a piece has been sewn on two sides, remove the pin.

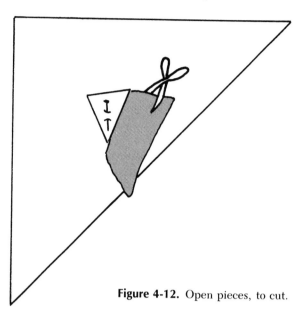

Figure 4-12. Open pieces, to cut.

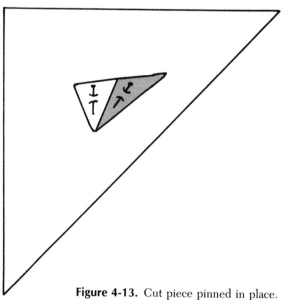

Figure 4-13. Cut piece pinned in place.

A potential problem is the formation of inside angles, indicated by the x's. To avoid this, stitch only as far as the bottom fabric extends and then cut within the lines that would be formed if the edges of the pieced section were extended, indicated by the dotted lines (Figure 4-14). Any cut on or within the boundaries formed by these lines will avoid an inside angle (Figure 4-15).

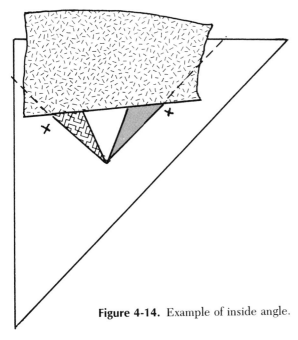

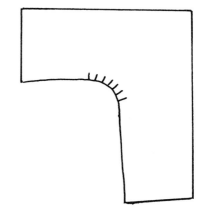

Figure 4-16. Fabric cut and clipped for curve.

place, trimming any excess seam allowance (Figure 4-17). Cut the fabric to the desired shape, avoiding inside angles.

Figure 4-14. Example of inside angle.

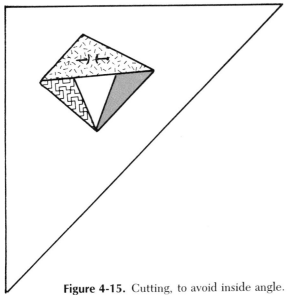

Figure 4-15. Cutting, to avoid inside angle.

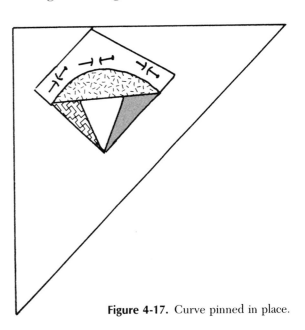

Figure 4-17. Curve pinned in place.

To form a curve, cut a right angle and clip the angle so that the seam allowance will lie flat (Figure 4-16). Turn under the clipped area and pin it over a pieced section. Turn the seam allowance along the rest of the fabric until it lies flat and forms a smoothly rounded curve. Pin in

Curves can also be cut after fabric has been stitched in place (Figure 4-18). Cut a piece of fabric to fit under the curve. Turn under the seam allowance on the curve and pin in place. Pins are left in the curves until the piecing is complete. Then the curves are appliquéd or stitched down with any embellishment desired.

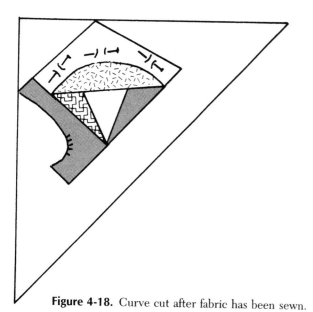

Figure 4-18. Curve cut after fabric has been sewn.

Chromania Too Piecing Directions

1. Draw an $8\frac{1}{2}''$ square on tracing paper. Using curved lines, divide it into nine patches roughly following Figure 4-19. Number as shown and cut apart. Using a single fabric, crazy piece each of the foundations with a different color. Extend the piecing at least $\frac{1}{4}''$ beyond the foundation to form a seam allowance. Trim the fabric evenly $\frac{1}{4}''$ from the edge of the foundation (Figure 4-20).

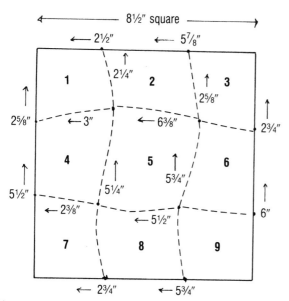

Figure 4-19. Division of square into a curved Nine-Patch.

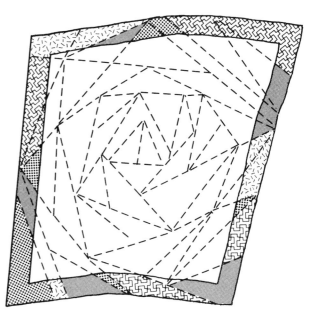

Figure 4-20. Foundation with $\frac{1}{4}''$ seam allowance on outside edges.

2. Use the edges of the foundations as a stitching guide, and piece the blocks together in numerical order into three rows of three blocks each.

3. Cut two 6 inch squares of freezer paper diagonally to form four triangles. Crazy piece with the grey print fabrics, stitching beyond the foundation to form a $\frac{1}{4}$ inch seam allowance. Trim, and sew on each side of the Nine Patch making Nine Patch-on-point (Figure 4-21).

Figure 4-21. Construction detail, with interior foundations partly removed.

4. For the border, make plastic templates from A and B (Figure 4-22). Add at least $\frac{1}{4}''$ seam allowance when cutting the fabric. Select seven of the nine colors used in the Nine Patch and cut four of each color from Template A. Cut 28 solid grey triangles from Template B (or eliminate Template B and cut seven $3\frac{1}{4}''$ squares diagonally twice to form the twenty-eight triangles).

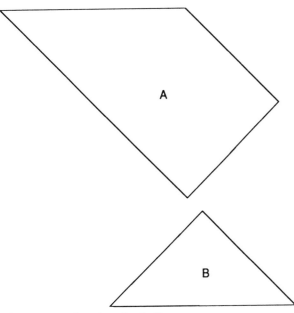

Figure 4-22. Template for A, B.

5. Using the layout (Figure 4-9) as a guide, trace each pieced border pattern (Figure 4-23) onto a foundation, repeating as necessary and positioning the corners as shown in Figure 4-9. To avoid confusion, write the location of each color directly onto the foundation. Using *under* pressed-piecing, start at the A end of the border and follow the pattern, piecing toward the B corner. This will result in a reversed pattern, which is not important as long as all four sides are sewn consistently (Figure 4-24). When the borders are pieced, trim any fabric that extends more than $\frac{1}{4}''$ beyond the foundation.

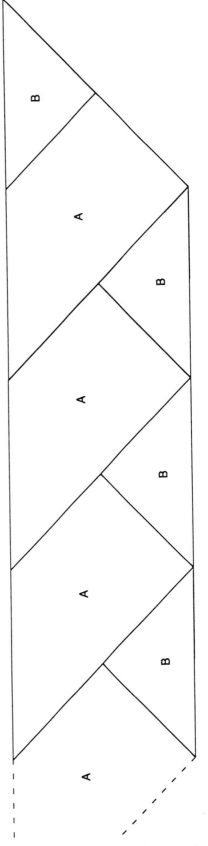

Figure 4-23. Border pattern for foundation marking.

Figure 4-24. Border and reverse, showing mirror-image.

6. Sew on the borders, lining up the center of each border with the central motif and using the foundation edges as stitching guides. Do not stitch across the seam allowances either when sewing on the borders or when mitering the corners. Remove the foundations and press lightly.

7. Baste, quilt and bind with navy. The Nine Patch piecing is quilted "in the ditch;" the triangles are quilted with half-circles radiating from the center $\frac{1}{2}''$ apart; and the border is quilted by echoing its pieced pattern outlines through the centers of the pieced elements.

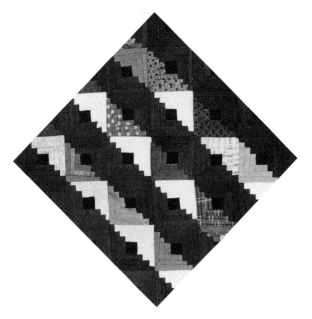

CHAPTER 5

The Log Cabin Family

Since this pattern appeared in the last half of the nineteenth century, Log Cabin quilts consistently have been a favorite of quilters and non-quilters alike. The graphic quality of the pattern works well with a wide variety of fabrics and fits into any decorating style.

The Log Cabin family of patterns is based on strips sewn around a center, most commonly a square. The strips are traditionally uniform and the progression is controlled outwardly from the center. The graphic effect of these patterns is totally dependent on the placement of color values within the block. Color value is the contrast between light and dark and is relative rather than absolute. Each color value is influenced by neighboring colors, appearing darker or lighter in contrast.

Log Cabin blocks can also be based on center shapes such as triangles, diamonds, hexagons and octagons. Blocks thus pieced can have three, four, six, or eight sides.

The basic four-sided Log Cabin takes two distinct forms. The first alternates placement of two light strips and two dark strips. This produces a diagonal separation of the color values across the block (Figure 5-1). Multiple blocks can be turned and set to produce a myriad of designs with colorful names such as Barn Raising (Figure 5-2), Straight Furrow (Figure 5-3), Sunshine and Shadow (Figure 5-4), and Streak of Lightning.

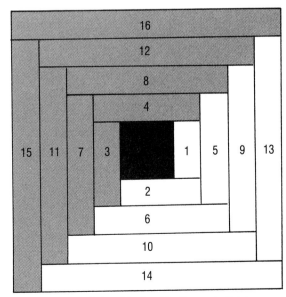

Figure 5-1. Log Cabin block with diagonal division.

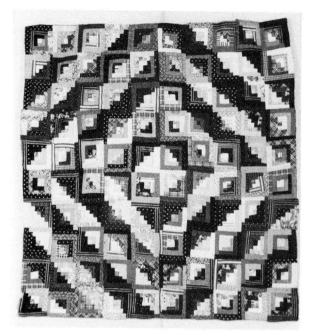

Figure 5-2. Antique Log Cabin quilt top with Barn Raising set.

Figure 5-3. Antique Log Cabin quilt top with Straight Furrow set.

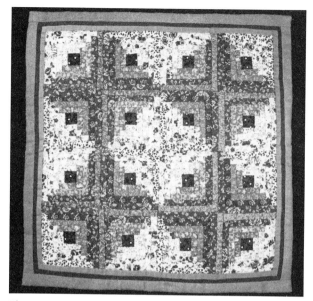

Figure 5-4. Miniature Log Cabin quilt with Sunshine and Shadow set.

The second major Log Cabin format, known as Courthouse Steps, divides the lights and darks horizontally and vertically, alternating the placement of pairs of light and dark fabric (Figure 5-5). The completed block exhibits an hourglass shape which, when combined with similar blocks, forms shapes like Japanese lanterns.

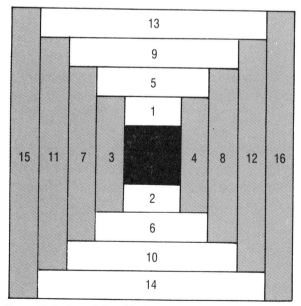

Figure 5-5. Log Cabin block with Courthouse Steps division.

The Pineapple is an eight-sided Log Cabin, pieced within a square block, with strips placed around the center on the horizontal, vertical and diagonal planes. The classic Pineapple uses light values for the horizontal-vertical planes and dark values for the diagonal planes (Figure 5-6). This produces an "X" figure in the finished block, which when joined to other blocks creates pineapple shapes as well as a great deal of circular movement (Figure 5-7). A common variation of the Pineapple coloration reverses the classic color arrangement putting the dark values on the horizontal-vertical planes and the light on the diagonal (Figure 5-8). This is seen in many old quilts, using black for the horizontal-vertical planes.

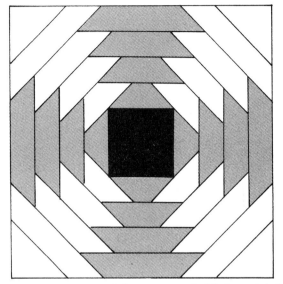

Figure 5-8. Variation of classic Pineapple block, with light on the diagonal planes.

Because center-based patterns can become distorted easily as the piecing progresses, the advantage of working on a stabilizing foundation became apparent early. Although utility fabric usually was used for foundations, it is still a testimony to the effectiveness of foundations that quilters were willing to use the extra fabric required (Figure 5-9). This extra layer provided by the foundation probably contributed to the fact

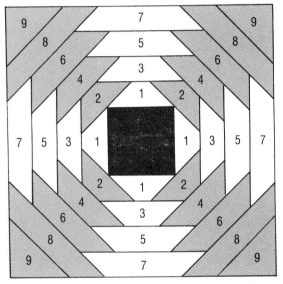

Figure 5-6. Classic Pineapple block, numbered with piecing order.

Figure 5-7. Four classic Pineapple blocks, set together.

Figure 5-9. Utility fabrics used as foundations.

that many old Log Cabin quilts were tied rather than quilted, since quilting through both the many seams and the foundation fabric was difficult (Figure 5-10).

Figure 5-10. Wool hexagon Log Cabin tied quilt.

Foundations continue to be an important element in contemporary Log Cabin work. The need varies with the shape and complexity of the pattern. A four-sided block with wide logs can be constructed with care without a foundation. As the logs become narrower and more numerous, or as variations involving other than four sides are made, a foundation becomes important, even essential.

In addition to stability, foundation use in these rigid lined patterns can help guarantee precision. A slight variation in seam allowance, often seen when blocks are pieced without a foundation, can result in problems when the blocks are joined. The piecing lines drawn on the foundation all but ensure the accuracy and integrity of the design.

Jane's miniature *Scrap Pineapple* quilt (Figure 5-11), resulted from a challenge to use difficult fabrics, including flannel shirts, satin, rayon, loosely woven cotton, and upholstery material. The combination of these fabrics with small blocks made foundations necessary.

Figure 5-11. Miniature *Scrap Pineapple*, 4″ blocks, using a wide variety of fabrics.

Columbia Gem (Figure 5-12) was made from blocks pieced in a Pineapple workshop. Preprinted foundation papers were used as foundations and the quilt was assembled from the wide variety of blocks and presented to Jane as a surprise. It is a testimony to the effectiveness of foundation piecing that fourteen different quilters could make blocks accurate enough to be combined into a single quilt.

Figure 5-12. *Columbia Gem*, from the collection of Jane Hall, Raleigh, N.C.

The choice between *top* or *under* pressed-piecing is based on individual preference. Either will work equally well with most Log Cabin foundation-based piecing. The few exceptions are obvious. A variation with pleated strips can only be accomplished from the *top*; small intricate blocks are pieced more accurately from *under* the foundation.

Sonja Shogren's small masterpiece *Opus One* (Color Plate 5), is constructed with incredibly small 1½″ Log Cabin blocks, having five logs on each side of the center. Lightweight paper was used as a foundation for precise marking and easy sewing with a small machine needle. The paper was left in place, becoming a permanent foundation, because of the difficulty of removing foundations on this scale. She used *under*

pressed-piecing to achieve accuracy, trimming the seam allowances closely.

This design category has great potential for innovative design. There are a number of elements that can be manipulated. Obviously, placement of color value within a block or between blocks creates a major focus. A foundation provides an invaluable design aid when making innovative departures from the basic color system of these patterns. Colors can be marked on the foundation to avoid confusion in the piecing process. This was essential in *Dawn's Early Light* (Color Plate 11) where the diagonal colors change and wash across the quilt from corner to corner. The effect is enhanced by the use of fifteen shades of black in the horizonal and vertical planes.

Mary Golden's quilt, *Ramblers* (Color Plate 6), uses both the traditional Log Cabin and the Courthouse Steps variation as well as the Pineapple to evoke the memory of her grandmother's house and rose garden. Using sharp value contrasts, she enhanced the barn-raising set with pieced houses and appliquéd rose vines.

Janet Elwin's *The Good Earth* (Color Plate 15) was made in honor of her mother and her mother's beautiful garden. Janet changes the shape of both the Log Cabin block and the strip widths within, which moves the middle of the block off-center. The hexagon shape and the bright flower colors make this innovative quilt reminiscent of an impressionistic Grandmother's Flower Garden.

The classic outlines of the Pineapple pattern were similarly altered with an off-center format in Jane's quilt, *Spinners* (Color Plate 31). This results in images of diamonds and ovals instead of the classic circles usually seen in a Pineapple quilt.

Fantasy Too, (Color Plate 23), by June Ryker not only changes the basic shape of a Log Cabin to a triangle, but also curves the usually straight strips. Two distinct blocks are used in the design, in different positions, each one having both inner and outer curved sides. June's innovative technique of piecing along a curved line with bias strips makes real the graphic illusion of circular movement often seen in this family of designs.

A foundation and *top* pressed-piecing are essential for June's bias curved piecing technique. In addition, after piecing, the block is checked for accuracy with a template of the finished size, to ensure that the bias strips lay flat and curve correctly.

Caryl Bryer Fallert used a free form approach to a Log Cabin format with a hexagon center in *Refraction #4-7* (Color Plate 16) which was pieced directly onto cotton batting. She created the illusion of swirling light emerging from dark with fabric dyed in both chromatic and value gradations.

The glow in Dixie's *Ora Pro Nobis* (Color Plate 12), achieved by grading colors, is accented by the simple addition of black setting strips. In *Iridescent Ripples* (Color Plate 13), a more subtle glow came from using one shiny fabric and capitalizing on the difference between the reflective properties of the warp and the weft threads.

Imaginative use of print fabric was combined with a Pineapple variation using uniform triangles on the diagonals by Jane in *Tori Forest* (Color Plate 14). This approaches the effect of a hybrid Log Cabin variation which uses squares or triangles in each row where the color values change (Figure 5-13).

Innovative design is not limited to contemporary quilts. This antique Pineapple Log Cabin quilt, (Color Plate 17) contains only traditional Pineapple blocks, hidden by the placement of the strong colors and plaids. A Courthouse Steps Log Cabin quilt (Color Plate 18) has blocks pieced on the diagonal rather than in the usual horizontal-vertical layout. The large corners resulting where the blocks meet gives the effect of a quasi-Pineapple pattern even though the quilt is a four-sided Log Cabin.

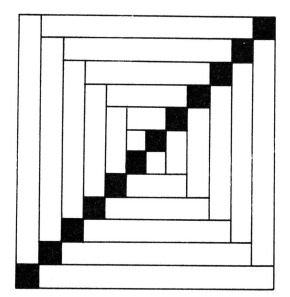 

Figure 5-13. Log Cabin with cornerstones (left) and Pineapple with Flying Geese diagonals.

■ Getting Started ■

Classic Pineapple Block

(Figure 5-14)

Figure 5-14. Pineapple block.

This 6-inch Pineapple block has dark color values on the diagonal planes and light on the horizontal. Trace the pattern onto tracing paper (Figure 5-15). Trace all the lines in one plane, before going on to the next plane. This is faster and more accurate than moving the pencil and the ruler along the lines of each row.

To practice the technique and the pattern, we suggest you use only two fabrics, one light and one dark. You will need a $1\frac{1}{2}''$ square of the dark for the center, and two $1''$ strips of each light and dark fabric, cut across the width of the yardage.

Either *top* or *under* pressed-piecing works well with this pattern. Remember that the dotted line is the fabric placement line for top pressed-piecing, and the solid line is the sewing line for under pressed-piecing. (See Chapter 2.)

Figure 5-15. Pineapple pattern marked with dotted lines for *top* piecing and solid lines for *under* piecing.

Beginning at the middle, pin the center square in place. To help keep the center squared, we piece the first two strips of light fabric on opposite sides. If you are using *top* pressed-piecing, the strip will be cut on the diagonal line (Figure 5-16*a*). If you are using *under* pressed-piecing, you will be using pre-cut strips that are not cut to shape at this point (Figure 5-16*b*). Repeat with the same fabric on the remaining sides of the center (Figures 5-17*a* and 5-17*b*).

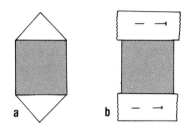

Figure 5-16 *a*. Opposite sides pieced onto center square, with *top* pressed-piecing. *b*. Opposite sides pieced onto center square, with *under* pressed-piecing.

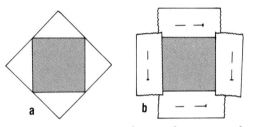

Figure 5-17 *a*. First row complete, with *top* pressed-piecing. *b*. First row of *under* pressed-piecing complete.

The second row is pieced on the diagonal plane and uses four dark strips, again sewn in 1–3, 2–4 order (Figures 5-18*a* and 5-18*b*).

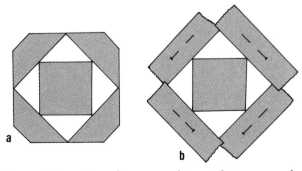

Figure 5-18 *a*. Second row complete, with *top* pressed-piecing. *b*. Second row complete, with *under* pressed-piecing.

Continue to piece rows of four lights, then four darks, until the corner is reached. After the third row, you do not need to piece on alternate sides. The final four dark pieces, in the corners, will be wider than the usual strip. They can be formed from a 2″ strip of fabric, or from two 3″ squares cut in half diagonally to form four triangles.

Once you have mastered the basic block, there are many variations in size and colorations you may wish to try. Remember that the graphic qualities of this pattern emerge and multiply when it is combined with other similar blocks.

White Collar
by Mary Golden
(Color Plate 29)

This quilt honors the white collar worker. The traditional House block can be a courthouse for the lawyer, a post office for the postal employee, an office building for the executive, or a school for the teacher. This project is especially personal when outgrown or out-moded clothing is used (Figure 5-19).

Silks, wools and shirtings can cause problems when combined with conventional piecing methods. Mary used *under* pressed-piecing for her quilt, which controlled the difficult fabrics and resulted in accurate piecing.

The *tie* blocks are pure Log Cabin Courthouse Steps, and the *building* blocks which resemble the traditional House blocks are actually an adaptation of the same Log Cabin design.

Quilt Size: 28″ × 28″

Block Size: 8″ (9 blocks)

Materials
Three wool trousers: a dark value, a medium-dark value, and a medium value
5–7 silk ties
1–3 shirts
Coordinated cotton backing, thin batting.
Borders: Medium value wool; cut two strips 2½″ × 28½″; two strips 2½″ × 24½″

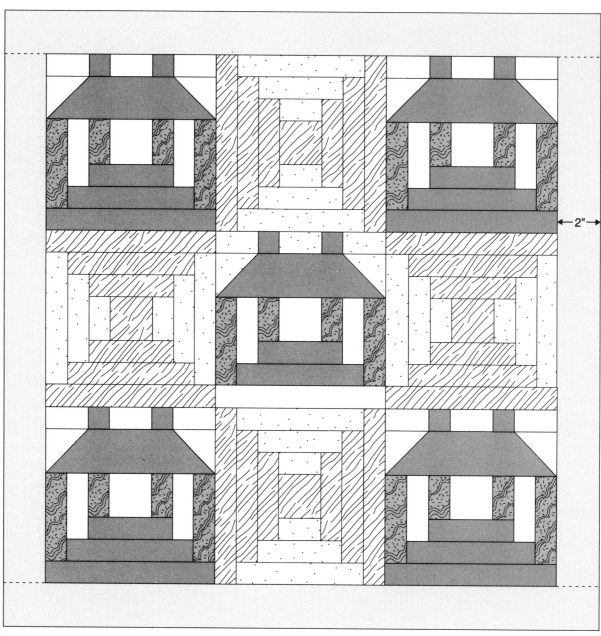

Figure 5-19. *White Collar* quilt layout.

Preparation

Coordinate these clothes as if dressing for a day at the office. Seam rip and press all fabrics. Use the wool steam setting on your iron and press on a bath towel.

Cutting Directions

Cut the largest and longest pieces first. Specific directions are given below. Pin together and label each group of pieces for each part of the blocks as they are cut.

Binding

Ties: cut four strips of freezer paper, $1\frac{1}{4}'' \times 30''$ and press onto the wrong sides of four different ties. Cut one long side of each tie flush with the freezer paper, and the other $\frac{1}{4}''$ outside the edge of the paper, making the tie strip $1\frac{1}{2}''$ wide.

Building Blocks (makes five):

Dark value wool: Roof—cut a $2\frac{3}{4}''$ strip and from that, cut five shapes with angled sides (Figure 5-20). Steps—cut four, $1\frac{3}{4}'' \times 8\frac{1}{2}''$; five, $1\frac{3}{4}'' \times 6\frac{1}{2}''$; five, $1\frac{3}{4}'' \times 4\frac{1}{2}''$.

Medium-dark value wool: Pillars—cut ten, $1\frac{3}{4}'' \times 4\frac{1}{2}''$; ten, $1\frac{3}{4}'' \times 2\frac{1}{2}''$. Chimneys—cut two, $1\frac{1}{2}'' \times 10$ inches.

Medium value wool: Building interior—cut five, $2\frac{3}{4}''$ squares; ten, $1\frac{3}{4}'' \times 3\frac{1}{2}''$.

Shirting: For the last step in the center building block—cut one, $1\frac{3}{4}'' \times 8\frac{1}{2}''$. Sky—cut three, $2\frac{1}{2}'' \times 10''$; five $3''$ squares, cut in half diagonally.

Tie Blocks (makes four):

Ties: Cut four, $2\frac{3}{4}''$ squares; eight, $1\frac{3}{4}'' \times 8\frac{1}{2}''$; eight, $1\frac{3}{4}'' \times 6\frac{1}{2}''$; eight, $1\frac{3}{4}'' \times 4\frac{1}{2}''$.

Shirting: Cut eight, $1\frac{3}{4}'' \times 6\frac{1}{2}''$; eight, $1\frac{3}{4}'' \times 4\frac{1}{2}''$; eight, $1\frac{3}{4}'' \times 2\frac{1}{2}''$.

Construction Directions

1. Stitch the ten inch lengths of sky-chimney-sky-chimney-sky together with a $\frac{1}{4}''$ seam allowance. Press the seams toward the chimneys. Cut across the panel into $1\frac{3}{4}''$ widths (Figure 5-21).

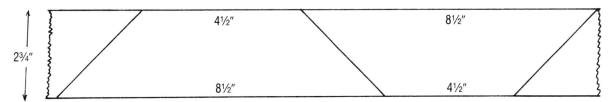

Figure 5-20. Cutting diagram for roof pieces.

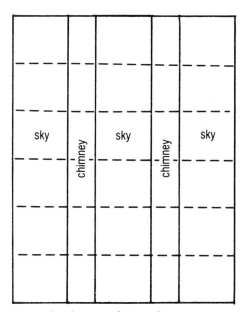

Figure 5-21. Sky-chimney-sky panel.

Note that the sky in the center *building* block is different from the others. It uses the same shirting as used in the *tie* blocks. It will need to be constructed separately if you want this effect.

2. Trace five *building* blocks (Figure 5-22) onto paper. Piece the block following the piecing order (Figure 5-23). Place the center square right side up on the undrawn side and secure lightly with a glue stick. Place the shortest pillar pieces right side down, aligned with the center square and pin where they overlap in the middle. Turn to the drawn side of the foundation and stitch with *under* pressed-piecing. Open to the right sides and press on a towel using a wool steam iron setting. Note: $\frac{3}{8}''$ is allowed for all seams except the chimney-sky row. Trim excess fabric as needed after stitching each seam.

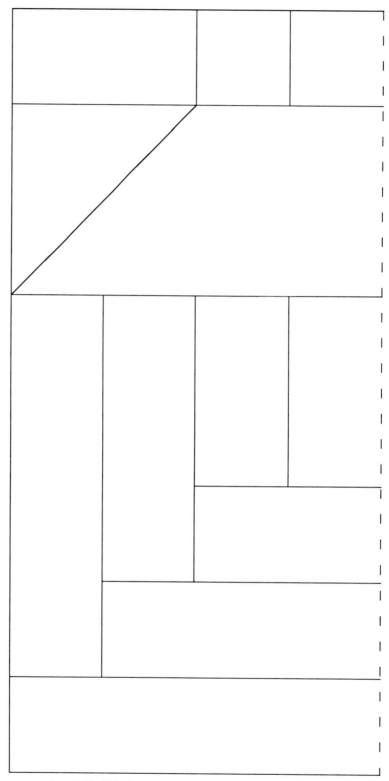

Figure 5-22. *Building* pattern. One-half of block.

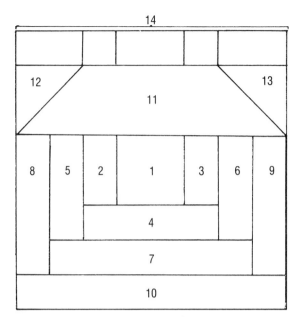

Figure 5-23. Piecing order for *building* pattern.

3. Continue piecing the bottom half of the block from the underside until the pillars, interiors and steps are sewn. One block, which will be in the center of the quilt, has light shirting for the final long step. Add the roof, followed by the sky triangles. Finally, pin the outer sides of the chimneys to the corners of the roofs. Pin the ends of the strip and sew. Press open and pin flat to the foundation, temporarily.

4. Trace four *tie* blocks (Figure 5-24) onto paper. Piece the blocks, following the piecing order (Figure 5-25). Secure the center square in place. Starting with the shirt rows, use *under* pressed-piecing to construct the block. Sew shirting strips 2 and 3 onto opposite sides of the center. Complete the square with tie strips 4 and 5 on the remaining opposite sides of the center. Continue alternating shirt and tie rows until the foundation is covered.

5. Trim all nine blocks $\frac{1}{4}''$ outside the drawn line. Each block should measure $8\frac{1}{2}''$. Following the layout (Figure 5-19), sew the blocks together in rows of three, and then sew the rows together. Remember that the *building* block with the shirting step goes in the center. Notice that the *tie* blocks are turned around the center.

6. Add the borders, sewing with the block side on top. Baste. Mary quilted "in the ditch" by machine. Bind with the freezer paper-backed ties, using one tie along each side. Attach the edge of the binding with the freezer paper on to the edge of the quilt, and sew through the freezer paper. Miter the corners by drawing the miter triangle onto the freezer paper; stitch. (See Chapter 8.) Press the outside $\frac{1}{4}''$ of the binding over the freezer paper to provide a crisp line for the fold. Remove the paper and stitch the binding closed.

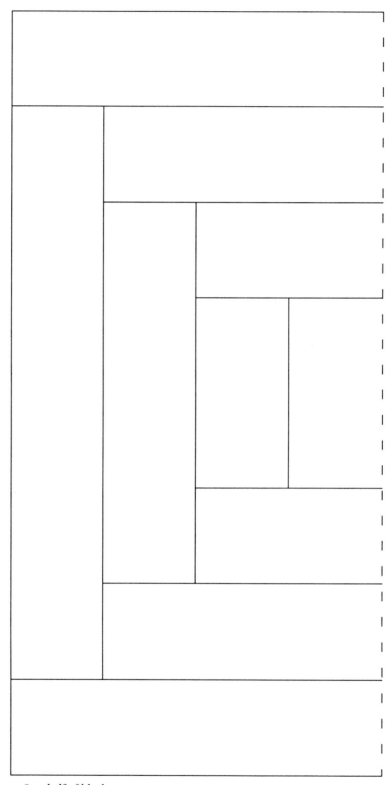

Figure 5-24. *Tie* pattern. One-half of block.

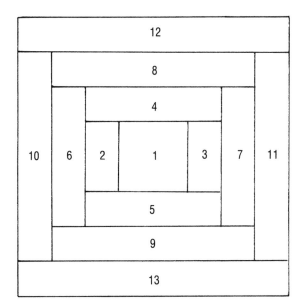

Figure 5-25. Piecing order for *tie* pattern.

Blueberries and Cream
by Janet Elwin
(Color Plate 30)

This project uses a hexagon centered Log Cabin which creates a six-sided block. Controlling the colors produces an interesting and unusual graphic design (Figure 5-26). The blocks are *under* press-pieced, and then are joined with seam-to-seam piecing.

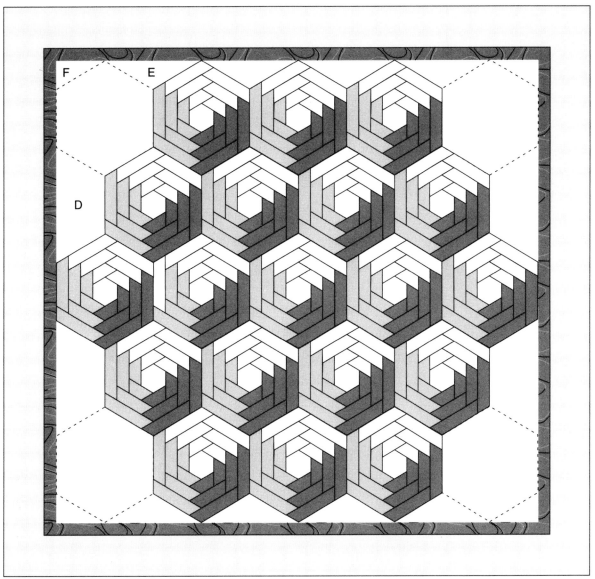

Figure 5-26. *Blueberries and Cream* quilt layout.

Ordinary paper can be used. If you have access to an accurate copy machine, it is possible to eliminate the tracing process. It is vital to measure the copied block, however, since it may well be shortened in one or both directions, which makes accurate joining with other blocks difficult.

Quilt Size: 34" × 36"

Block Size: 7" hexagon Log Cabin (19 blocks)

Materials

10 fabrics for the hexagons, prints or solids:
  $\frac{1}{4}$ yard fabric for center hexagons.
  $\frac{1}{8}$ yd each of 2 lights, 2 mediums, 2 darks, for Rows A and B
  $\frac{1}{4}$ yd each of 1 light, 1 medium, 1 dark, for Row C
  $\frac{1}{2}$ yd of background fabric
  $\frac{1}{4}$ yd dark fabric for Border #1
  $\frac{1}{2}$ yd light fabric for Border #2
  1 yd navy backing fabric, batting.
Template plastic; paper for patterns

Construction Directions

1. Copy or trace the hexagon pattern (Figure 5-27) carefully onto paper. Be sure to include the marked notch on Rows A-1, B-1 and C-1. You will need 19 identical patterns. Cut the patterns on the outside lines; these will be the finished sizes. Number the logs as shown.

2. Make a plastic template for the center hexagon from Figure 5-27. Cut 19 hexagons from fabric, adding a seam allowance. Janet suggests using a larger than normal seam allowance, $\frac{1}{2}$", to be certain that the shape will cover the lines adequately. Cut the light, medium and dark fabrics for Rows A, B, and C, into strips $1\frac{1}{4}$" wide across the width of the fabric.

3. On the undrawn or "wrong" side of the paper pattern, arrange the fabric hexagon to cover all the lines of the printed hexagon. Place the wrong side of the fabric against the wrong side of the paper, right side of the fabric facing outward. When arranging the fabric, it helps to hold the printed pattern facing you, with the reverse side towards a light or a window. Pin the hexagon in place and stitch along the lines of the shape (Figure 5-28).

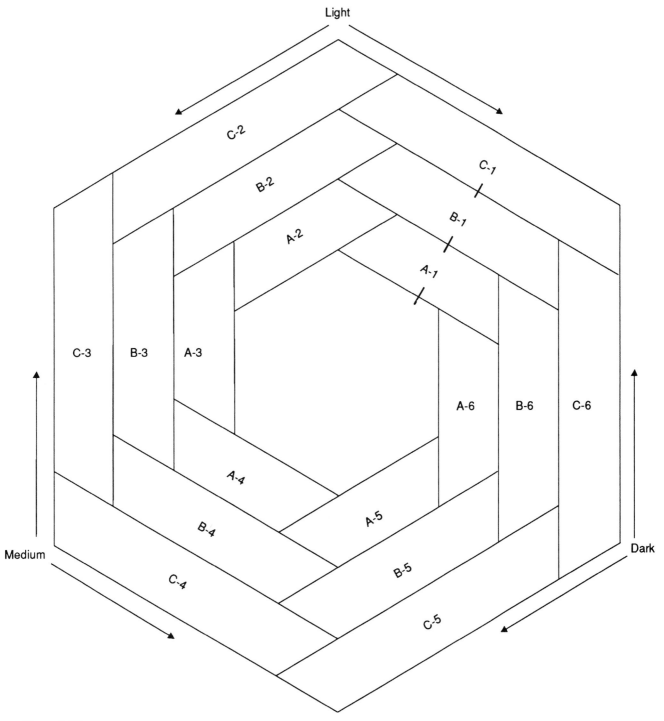

Figure 5-27. Hexagon pattern.

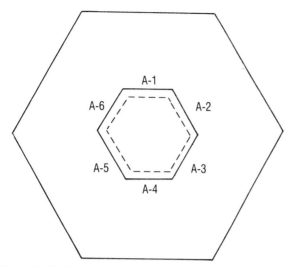

Figure 5-28. Center hexagon stitched in place under foundation.

4. With the right side of the light strip facing the right side of the hexagon, line up strip A-1 with the cut edge of the hexagon, covering the stitching line of log A-1 with $\frac{1}{4}''$ seam allowance. Note the notches on all the Log 1 sections. Turn to the drawn side of the paper and stitch on the line towards the notch. Stop at the notch, leaving the remainder of the A-1 strip free (Figure 5-29).

5. Cut the fabric strip, making sure that it covers the log, A-1. Finger press the strip away from the center to cover A-1. Pin the loose end of the log in place, to hold the fabric strip straight (Figure 5-30).

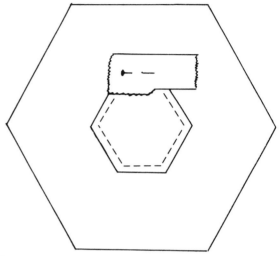

Figure 5-30. First strip opened and pinned in place, showing loose end.

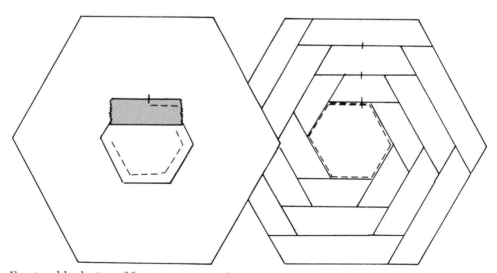

Figure 5-29. Front and back view of first strip sewn in place.

6. With another strip of the same fabric, cover Log A-2, matching the cut edge of the hexagon side, turning the paper over, and stitching on the line from the drawn side (Figure 5-31). Cut the strip, trim any excess fabric caught under the seam, finger press the strip up, and pin.

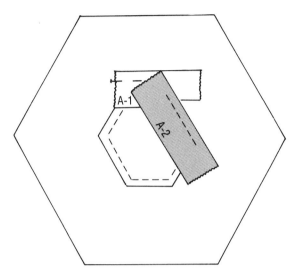

Figure 5-31. Second strip sewn in place.

7. Repeat the process for Logs A-3 and A-4 with dark value fabrics and Logs A-5 and A-6 with medium value fabrics. Before stitching Log A-6, pin back the free fabric on Log A-1 (Figure 5-32). Remove the pin after stitching A-6.

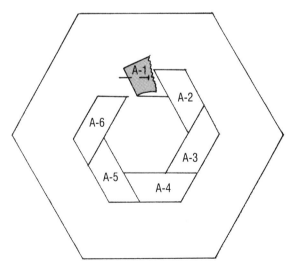

Figure 5-32. A-1 strip pinned back before A-6 strip is sewn.

8. In order to stitch the remaining section of Log A-1, rip back the stitched fabric *from the paper only* on Log A-1 and a portion of Log A-2. This allows you to fold down Log A-1, arrange the fabric strip to cover the end of A-6, and sew the unstitched portion of A-1, from the notch to the end (Figure 5-33). Releasing the stitching from the paper only leaves fabric strips A-1 and A-2 sewn together.

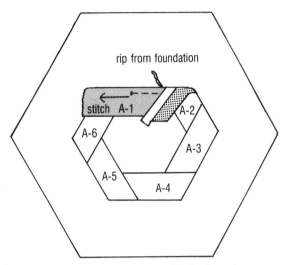

Figure 5-33. A-1 strip in position for final stitching.

9. Finger press strips A-1 and A-2 back in place. This completes Row 1.

10. Repeat these instructions for the second and third rows. Use the next set of light, dark and medium fabrics for the second row (B) and the third set for the third row (C).

11. When the hexagon is complete, press it. Trim the excess fabric from along the edges to a $\frac{1}{4}''$ seam allowance all around the block. At this point Janet prefers to mark a $\frac{1}{4}''$ sewing line around the outside of the block, and remove the paper. You also have the option of leaving the paper on the outside logs in place to serve as a stitching guide.

12. Arrange the hexagon Log Cabin blocks as shown in Figure 5-26. Make plastic templates from D, E, F (Figure 5-34) and the hexagon block pattern (Figure 5-27), for the background pieces, adding $\frac{1}{4}''$ seam allowances. Use the templates to

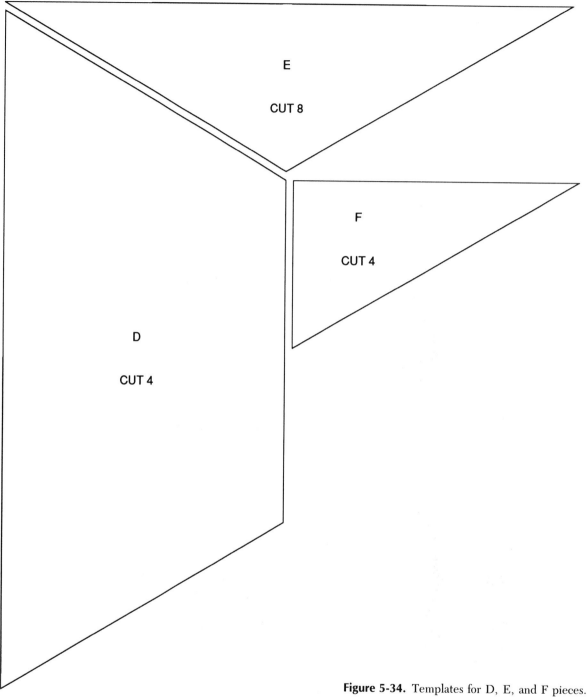

Figure 5-34. Templates for D, E, and F pieces.

cut four hexagons, and D, E, and F as indicated from the background fabric. Stitch the quilt together in rows, with seam-to-seam piecing, using the various shapes to square off the design into a rectangle 29″ × 31″.

13. For the inner border, cut two pieces 1″ × 29½″, and two pieces 1″ × 31½″. Stitch onto the appropriate sides of the quilt top and miter the corners. (See Chapter 8.) For the second border,

cut two pieces 3″ × 34½″ and two pieces 3″ × 36½″, stitch and miter as before.

14. Cut the backing fabric 2½″ larger than the quilt top on all sides. Mark the quilting designs, baste the layers together and quilt. Janet quilted over the hexagons using variegated blue and white thread, in a clamshell design. She finished the quilt with a separate binding made from the fabric used for the final border.

Spinners
by Jane Hall
(Color Plate 31)

After making a classic Pineapple block, it is intriguing to work on a Pineapple Log Cabin with the center not in the middle of the block. This block has a 1″ center, with the strips on one corner (one horizontal, one diagonal and one vertical plane) finishing $\frac{1}{4}$″ wide. The strips on the opposite corner (one horizontal, one diagonal and one vertical plane) finish at $\frac{1}{2}$″ wide. The remaining two diagonal strips are approximately $\frac{3}{8}$″.

This arrangement shifts the focus of the pattern, and changes the design. The project shown has 16 blocks (Figure 5-35), which gives space for repeats of the square, diamond and oval shapes formed. Four blocks would produce a small piece with more limited graphics.

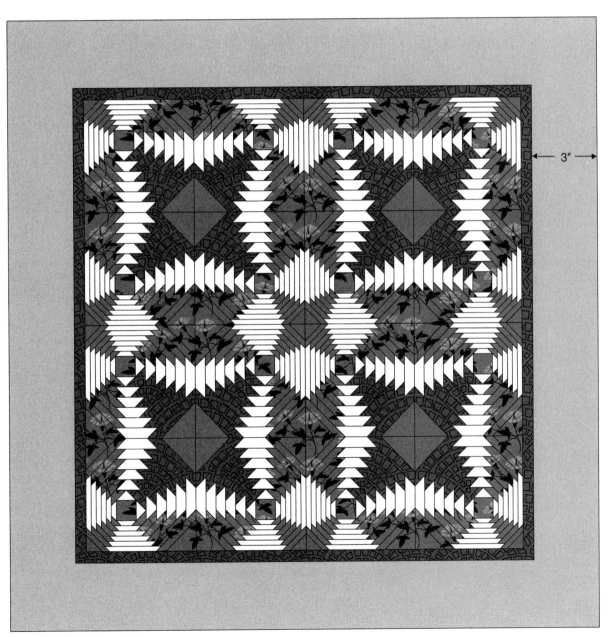

Figure 5-35 *Spinners* quilt layout.

Quilt Size: 28″ × 28″

Block Size: 5½″ (16 blocks)

Materials

¾ yd color #1 (medium blue)
¾ yd color #2 (dark blue)
1 yd color #3 (coordinating print)
1 yd background light color value solid or print-
   solid fabric
Backing fabric; batting; binding
Tracing paper

Construction Directions

1. Trace the pattern 16 times (Figure 5-36). To avoid the tedium of tracing, this is a good pattern to mark with needle punching. Trace the pattern onto typing paper. Pin this pattern to a stack of 8 sheets of tracing paper, and stitch with an unthreaded sewing machine, along the lines of each plane, in turn. Use a medium stitch length (10–12 per inch). This marks each line accurately, and the punctures serve to bind the stack of paper together so that it doesn't slip. The master tracing can be used again for another stack of patterns.

2. We suggest using *under* pressed-piecing because of the small strips and the many points. "A," "B," and "C" are differing widths of strips. On the pattern "A" signifies the horizontal, verti-

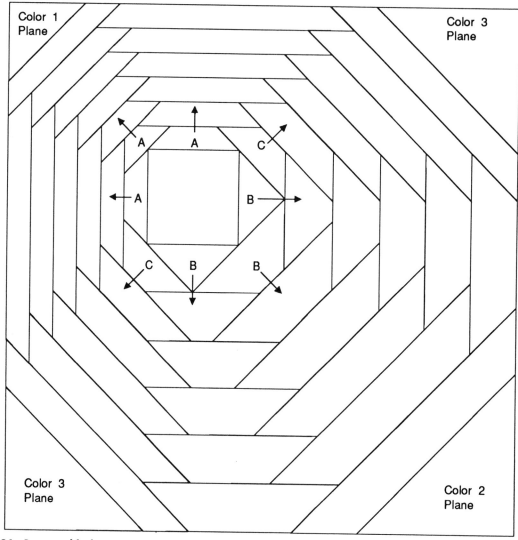

Figure 5-36. *Spinners* block pattern showing color placement.

cal, and diagonal planes that are composed of $\frac{1}{4}''$ strips; "B" the horizontal, vertical, and diagonal planes that are made of $\frac{1}{2}''$ strips; and "C" the remaining two diagonal planes. All the horizontal-vertical planes are the same background color. Mark color placement #1, #2, and #3 on the appropriate diagonal planes of the paper pattern to avoid confusion while piecing. Remember that you are working in mirror image and that the colors can easily be reversed inadvertently. Mark all of the blocks at the same time so that none of them are marked on the wrong side and reversed.

3. Cut strips across the width of the fabric as follows: 6 strips of Color #1, $\frac{3}{4}''$ wide; 9 strips of Color #2, one inch wide; 15 strips of Color #3, one inch wide; 15 strips of background, $\frac{3}{4}''$ wide (A) and 13 strips of background one inch wide (B). Cut $1\frac{1}{2}''$ center squares from Color #3.

4. For each block: pin a center square on a foundation, with the wrong side of the fabric against the paper. Make sure that the fabric covers the lines of the drawn or punched square, with an adequate seam allowance on all sides. Using the side of the square as a measure, cut off two pieces of the $\frac{3}{4}''$ wide light strip (A) and two pieces of the one inch wide light strip (B). These will surround the center square for the first row.

5. Lay an A strip onto the center square at the "A" sector, right sides together with cut edges lined up. Pin in place, turn the foundation over, and stitch on the line, beginning two stitches before and ending two stitches after the line ends. These extra stitches anchor the seam allowance and the strip until it is crossed by the next round of strips. Use a small stitch length, 12–14 per inch. Trim any excess seam allowance to a scant $\frac{1}{4}''$, press up the strip, and anchor with a pin.

6. Place a B strip on a side of the center square at the "B" sector opposite the A strip just sewn, and repeat the pinning, stitching and trimming process (Figure 5-37).

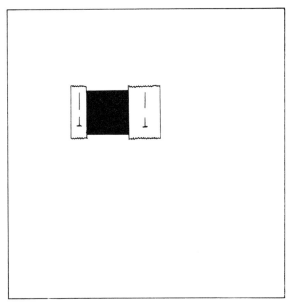

Figure 5-37. First two strips in place, on opposite sides of the center square.

7. Sew the second A strip and the second B strip as above. This completes Row 1 (Figure 5-38).

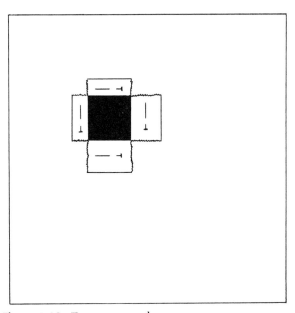

Figure 5-38. First row complete.

8. Using the stitching line for Row 2 as a guide, cut pieces of colors 1, 2 and 3 to match the appropriate lines in each plane with a generous $\frac{1}{4}''$ seam allowance on each end. The Color 1 strip will cover the line leading into the section marked "1" and will be placed right side down, against the sewn and pinned strips of Row 1. Pin in place, putting the pin low down in the strip so that it will not get caught in the feed dogs during the stitching. Make sure that the strip is straight with the lines of that plane, and that there is an adequate seam allowance. Stitch, trim and pin as before. Sew Color 2 next, opposite Color 1. Then add the two Color 3 strips (Figure 5-39).

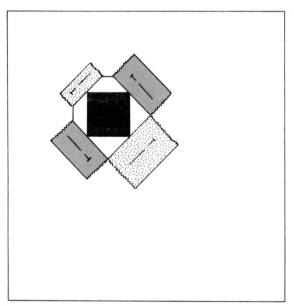

Figure 5-39. Second row complete.

9. Continue sewing rows, alternating background A and B with colors 1, 2, and 3. By Row 5, you should be able to pin strips for the entire row, and stitch around the row without breaking the thread, lifting the presser foot at the end of each row. It is absolutely essential to trim each strip and pin it up securely before proceeding to the next strip. Pressing each row as it is completed helps keep the block flat.

10. The corners are made by cutting wider strips of each fabric. For Color 1, cut a strip $1\frac{1}{2}''$ wide; for color 2, cut a strip $2''$ wide; for color 3, cut a strip $1\frac{3}{4}''$ wide.

11. After the sewing is complete, press the block, and sew a line of stay-stitching $\frac{1}{4}''$ outside the final line of the block. Trim all fabric and paper to that stitched line (Figure 5-40). Do not remove the paper at this juncture; the outer drawn or punched line serves as a sewing line for assembling the blocks.

Figure 5-40. Completed block, showing stay-stitching at edge.

12. When all blocks have been sewn, you must decide on the arrangement for the quilt. Where the thinnest planes meet (color 1), diamond shapes will be formed. Where the thickest planes meet (color 2), squares will be formed. And where color 3 meets color 3, ovals will form. It is possible to place these shapes in several combinations within the framework of 16 blocks.

13. Sew the blocks together in rows, matching the lines and points exactly. It is easy to stitch accurately with the paper to guide you. To make the joins, put two blocks together, right sides facing. Stab a pin at the first point in the first block and stick it through the second block at exactly that same point (Figure 5-41). Pin vertically and match the next points. Open the matched seams to double check that the points are in line. A perfect chevron should be formed (Figure 5-42).

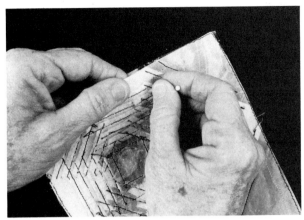

Figure 5-41. Stabbing pins at joining points of two blocks.

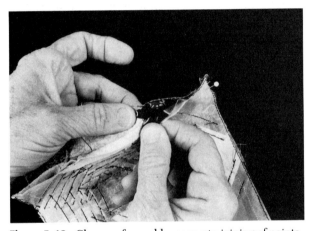

Figure 5-42. Chevron formed by accurate joining of points.

14. Cut inner borders and binding from Color #2. Inner border strips should be 1 inch × 24 inches, each sewn onto one side of the quilt, exactly on the drawn outer line of the blocks. Miter the corners and press the seams into the border. (See Chapter 8.)

15. The outer border is cut from Color #1: four strips, $3\frac{1}{2}''$ × 30". In sewing to a small strip where wobbles would be noticeable, it is easier to keep the stitching line straight if you gauge it by the previous line of stitching, rather than by the cut edges. Press this seam into the outer border, and miter the corners.

16. Baste, quilt, and bind with color #2. Corners and centers were quilted "in-the-ditch." Shapes such as diamonds or squares were quilted around to emphasize them. A compass and pencil or chalk were used to mark the quilting lines. Curved and straight lines quilted within the color figures serve to flatten and enhance the design.

17. Bind with a continuous straight binding, cut from Color #2. You will need three strips cut across the width, $1\frac{1}{4}$ inches wide for a narrow binding.

CHAPTER 6

Other Traditional Patterns

Many favorite quilt patterns haven't been considered for foundation piecing, for two reasons. First there is no need to add a foundation for either stability or precision in many patterns. Second when there might be such a need, the geometry of the pattern often precludes a pressed-piecing process.

There are many cases, however, when there would be an advantage to piecing on a foundation. The stability of a foundation can be invaluable when using fabrics that ravel, slip or stretch; or when cutting off-grain to take advantage of a printed fabric. With patterns that are difficult to piece accurately due to the shapes of the pattern pieces and the necessity to match multiple points, foundations can assure precision piecing. Miniature blocks are another example where foundations are helpful. Their tiny pieces are worth the effort of preparing a foundation for the sake of the accuracy gained.

Finally, in many cases, blocks or segments can be pieced faster by pressed-piecing on a foundation than with seam-to-seam piecing in the conventional way. There is no need to pin and match beginning and ending points since the line is there to provide an exact measure for sewing. With under foundation pressed-piecing, there is often no need to cut templates. Fabric pieces can be approximate rather than exactly sized since the sewing line will define the shape and any excess seam allowance will be trimmed.

Apart from the types of design categories we have already discussed in preceding chapters, other traditional blocks can be pieced in their entirety on a foundation. Friendship block (Figure 6-1), which builds from the center is such a block. Sailboat (Figure 6-2) and Crossed Canoes (Figure 6-3) are examples of diagonally-oriented blocks which are easily press-pieced. These latter two blocks are usually set together in groups of four, with a quarter-turn rotation. Foundation piecing aids and simplifies that construction.

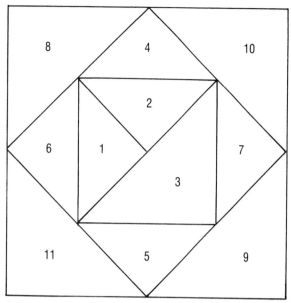

Figure 6-1. Friendship block, piecing progression.

With other blocks, although pressed piecing may be desirable, it does not appear to be feasible. Inside angles, crossed seams and sharp curves present obstacles to pressed piecing. However, if the pattern can be divided into segments that can be press-pieced, foundation work becomes possible.

It can provide the desired stability and precision for patterns such as Railroad Crossing, which tends to stretch during construction because of the many pieces and the diagonal set of the design (Figure 6-4). When four Railroad Crossing blocks are joined and rotated, (Figure 6-5), working in segments makes variations such as reversing the direction of the corner units in alternate blocks easy to plan and execute.

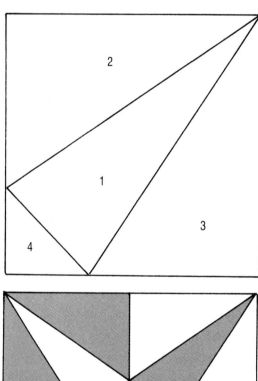

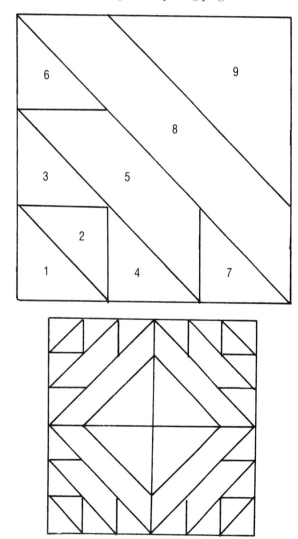

Figure 6-2. Sailboat block; four blocks set together.

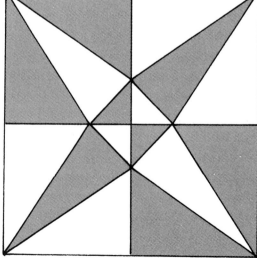

Figure 6-3. Crossed Canoes block; four blocks set together

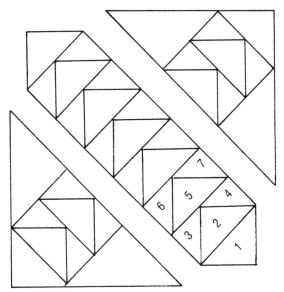

Figure 6-4. Railroad Crossing block, showing segment piecing order.

Figure 6-5. Railroad Crossing four-block layout with corners reversed on alternate blocks.

Designs which radiate from the center can be done in segments with precision and speed. These designs will need to be divided into halves, quarters or even eighths in order to use pressed-piecing. For example, Kaleidoscope can be press-pieced as segments in half-blocks (Figure 6-6).

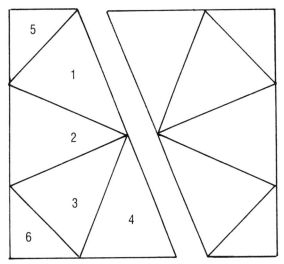

Figure 6-6. Kaleidoscope segments with piecing progression.

A circular design, inspired by a mosaic floor (Figure 6-7), would be daunting as a pieced pattern. Divided into twenty-four wedges, however, it could be press-pieced easily on foundations in segments, and joined with precision.

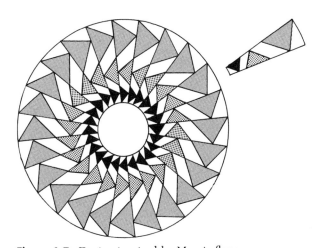

Figure 6-7. Design inspired by Mosaic floor.

In some instances, parts of a pattern can be press-pieced in segments but then must be combined with other kinds of piecing to complete the block. Dusty Miller, Sunburst, and Mariner's Compass are patterns which cannot be completely worked as press-pieced segments. The pieced arc and strip of New York Beauty (Figure 6-8) can be stabilized effortlessly in segments on a foundation. They are then joined to the other parts of the block with either single foundation or non-foundation piecing.

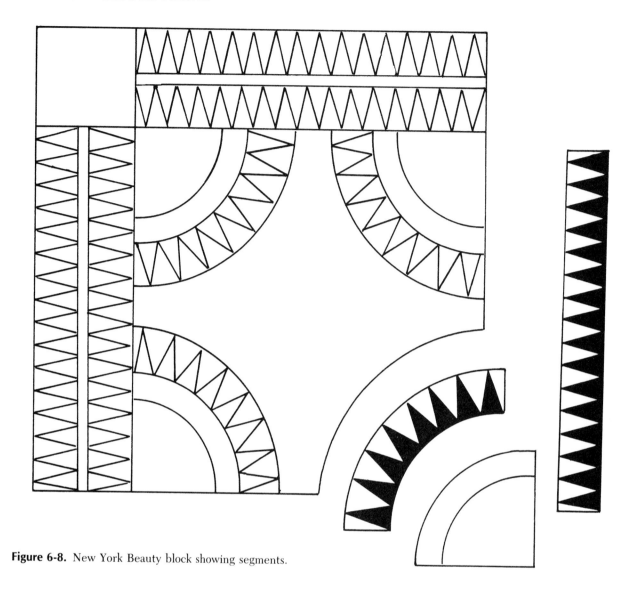

Figure 6-8. New York Beauty block showing segments.

In all of these designs, segments, single foundations and non-foundation pieces are joined with seam-to-seam piecing. The foundations generally remain in place until the block is completed; their edges become a guideline for sewing an accurate seam.

Dixie's quilt *Oak and Sumac* (Color Plate 19), is made with the Dusty Miller block. As we show in our Getting Started section, using foundations for the wedges made the construction of this 68 piece block fast and accurate. Like the Kaleidoscope and the Pineapple patterns, multiple blocks of this pattern create movement, secondary shapes, and strong graphics.

Joann Wilson's *Mariner's Compass* variation (Color Plate 20), is an exact replica of an antique quilt from the T. T. Wentworth Jr. State Museum in Pensacola, FL. The 5″ compasses were pieced

on paper, using *under* press-pieced segments like the Mariner's Compass project in our Getting Started section.

To construct the feathered stars and sawtooth border in *Peaceable Kingdom* (Figure 6-9), Debbie Hall used two foundation methods. She makes one inch squares of half-square triangles by *under* piecing on a foundation marked with both sewing and cutting lines (Figure 6-10). This foundation is placed on top of the two fabrics used and stitched on the sewing lines through all layers. After stitching it is cut apart, the paper is removed, and the squares are pressed open. To assemble the sawtooth segments for the stars, the pre-sewn squares and any other pieces needed to complete the segments are then *top* press-pieced onto a paper foundation.

Debbie says she always tries to find a paper

Figure 6-9. *Peaceable Kingdom* detail, Debbie Hall, Cincinnati, Ohio, 1990. Machine-pieced and quilted (trapunto) from original designs.

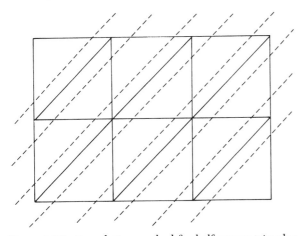

Figure 6-10. Foundation marked for half-square triangles.

method to sew the detailed elements in her quilts because of the ease and accuracy she can achieve. She makes dollhouse quilts with squares, strips, and curves, all on paper foundations. She makes her foundations by photocopying the pattern, taking care to use copy machines that are 100% accurate.

The books are full of other patterns that can be adapted easily to foundation work. As you become aware of the advantages of working on a foundation, you will look at traditional patterns with fresh eyes. To determine if a pattern is a candidate for foundation piecing, it is necessary to ask yourself several questions:

1. Is the fabric I want to use potentially troublesome?
2. Are there many small pieces that might be hard to handle?

3. Are points within the pattern difficult to match with precision?
4. Are there portions of the pattern that would stretch easily?
5. Are there multiple intersections to match when joining blocks?
6. Is there a logical way to break the pattern into segments that can be press-pieced?

If there is, give it a try.

■ Getting Started ■

Dusty Miller Block
(Figure 6-11)

Figure 6-11. Dusty Miller block.

Dusty Miller, a variation of Kaleidoscope, introduces segments combined with ordinary piecing. The four diagonal wedges containing many triangles, no two of which are alike, are press-pieced as segments. Using *under* pressed-piecing and chunks of fabric cut to approximate size, rather than cutting shapes from templates adds time-saving to the obvious precision and stability of foundation work. It is unnecessary and impractical to piece the horizontal-vertical wedges on foundations because of their curved parts, so they are constructed with ordinary seam-to-seam piecing (Figure 6-12).

1. Trace the four diagonal wedges (Figure 6-13) on tracing paper.

2. Make plastic templates of A, B, and C (Figure 6-14). Cut four each A and C from dark green fabric and four B from white fabric. Trace onto wrong sides of fabric, adding $\frac{1}{4}''$ seam allowance on all sides. Piece in traditional seam-to-seam manner.

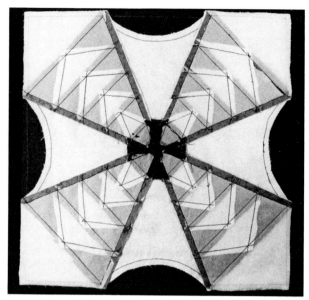

Figure 6-12. Reverse side of block, showing segments combined with ordinary piecing.

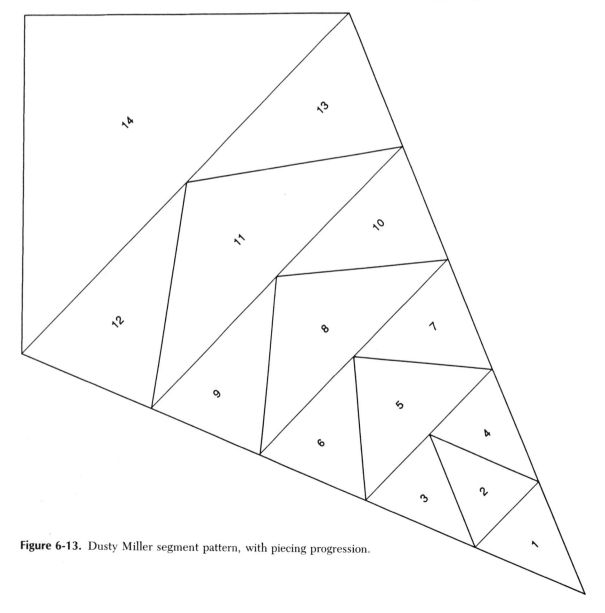

Figure 6-13. Dusty Miller segment pattern, with piecing progression.

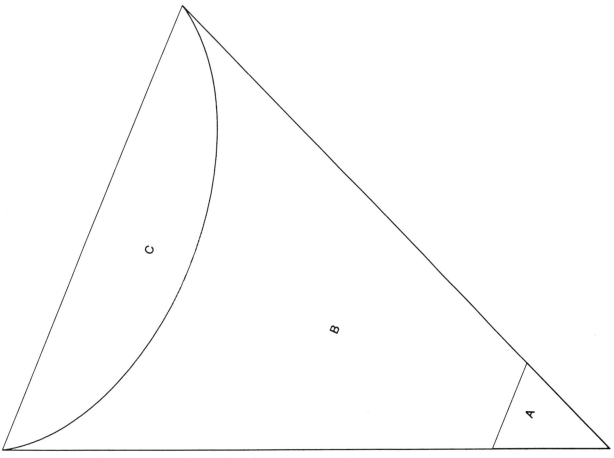

Figure 6-14. Templates for horizontal-vertical wedge pieces.

3. To make a diagonal wedge: pin a piece of dark green fabric right side up, onto the unmarked side of the foundation so that it will adequately cover Triangle #1. Lay a piece of white fabric over it, right sides together, and pin in place. Turn the foundation over and stitch on the line.

4. Turning back to the fabric side, trim the seam allowance to a scant $\frac{1}{4}''$, open the fabric and press. Lay a piece of medium green fabric on one side of the white triangle #2 just added, pin, turn over the foundation and stitch as before. Trim seam allowance and press open. Repeat for the other side of triangle #2. Continue the piecing process until each of the four wedges is complete. Trim, leaving $\frac{1}{4}''$ of fabric outside all edges of the foundations.

5. While you don't need to cut fabric from templates, it is helpful to have the fabric cut at the approximate angle of the shapes. This helps assure that the area is covered when the pieces are

opened. It also keeps the integrity of the grainline. The unsewn sides of the white triangles were roughly trimmed to size including seam allowance, after sewing and pressing. Use the drawn line of the pattern as a guide (Figure 6-15). The green background fabric for each side of the

Figure 6-15. Cutting the white triangle shape.

white triangles was roughly cut to size following the angle of the triangles before stitching in place (Figure 6-16).

6. Combine the press-pieced segments and the non-foundation pieced wedges into quarters and halves before joining into a block, following the construction diagram (Figure 6-17).

Like the Kaleidoscope and the Pineapple patterns, multiple blocks of this pattern create movement, secondary shapes, and strong graphics.

Figure 6-16. Cutting the green triangle shapes.

Figure 6-17. Block construction progression.

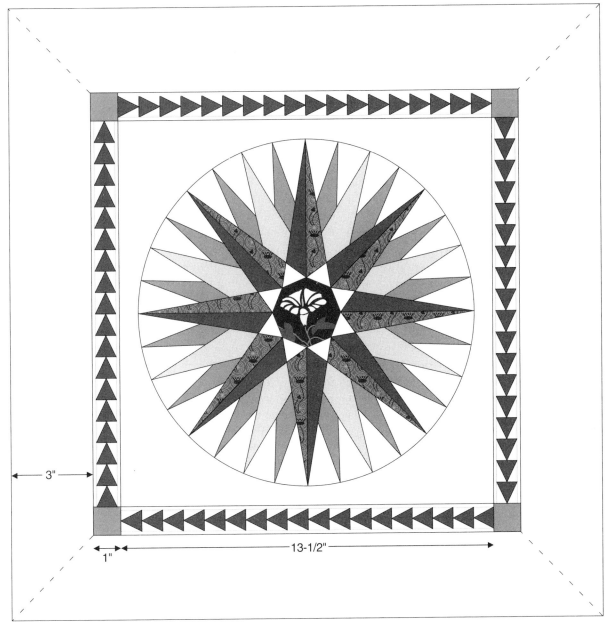

Figure 6-18. *Mariner's Compass* quilt layout.

Mariner's Compass
by Jane Hall
(Color Plate 32)

This traditional pattern with its fine tapered points and many intersections can be pieced easily and precisely using foundation techniques. It is a block which combines pressed-pieced segments with single foundation piecing. We used *under* pressed-piecing.

To make a small quilt, we constructed an Uzbek arrowhead border around a single complex Mariner's Compass block (Figure 6-18). Directions for the border are found in Chapter 8, Borders.

Quilt Size: $21\frac{1}{2}'' \times 21\frac{1}{2}''$

Block Size: $13\frac{1}{2}''$ (one block)

Materials
$\frac{1}{8}$ yd dark blue fabric for inner points, C, and Uzbek border

⅛ yd brown fabric
⅛ yd red fabric
Small amounts of pink, medium blue, and floral fabric (for center)
1 yd background fabric, solid or print that reads as solid
Backing fabric; batting; binding
Freezer paper; template plastic

Cutting Directions
From dark blue, cut 8 strips 1½″ × 5½″ for half of C points
From medium blue, cut 8 strips 1½″ × 5½″ for other half of C points
From pink, cut 8 1½″ squares for B points

From floral print, cut a circular shape large enough to cover the center octagon, centering a flower or design from the print on the piece.

Construction Directions
1. Draw a 12″ circle on the dull side of a square of freezer paper. Copy the Mariner's Compass pattern (Figure 6-19) rotating the pattern to fit it into the circle. Letter each point and section as shown to avoid confusion.

2. Trace the outer circle of this pattern onto the wrong side of a 14″ square of background fabric (Figure 6-20). Set aside until the Compass is pieced.

3. Make plastic templates without seam allowances for E and F from your master pattern (Figure 6-19). Trace and cut out 16 red E shapes and 32 background F shapes, keeping the grain con-

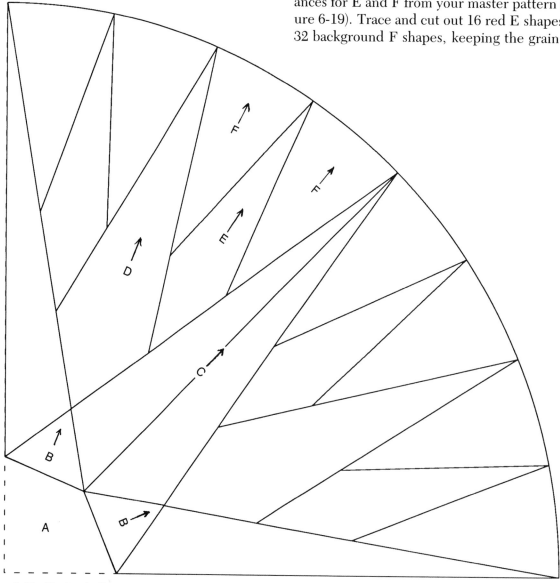

Figure 6-19. *Mariner's Compass* pattern. One-quarter of block.

Fold

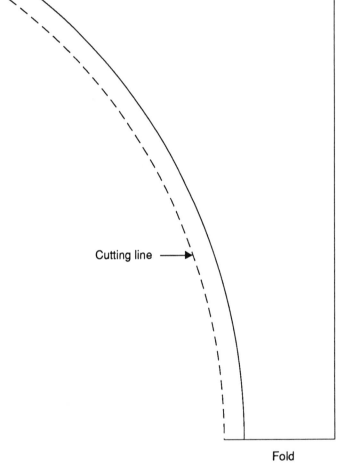

Cutting line ⟶

Fold

Figure 6-20. Pattern for outer circle, with seam allowance marked. One quarter of block.

sistent as shown by the arrows on the pattern (Figure 6-18). These are sewing line templates, so you must add $\frac{1}{4}''$ seam allowance on the fabric.

Because of the needle-sharp points and the necessity of keeping the integrity of the grainline of the background wedges, it is useful to cut exact shapes here, rather than dealing with chunks of fabric as we did in the Dusty Miller block.

4. The geometry of the pattern precludes press-piecing the entire pattern, but studying the block, you can readily see ways to press-piece some segments, providing accuracy and saving time.

5. Drawing the entire block on freezer paper provides foundations for all the piecing. Cut the block apart, into segment foundations and single foundations as follows: the outside segments, F-E-F, points C (entire point), and points D. Leave the eight B triangles attached to the center octagon A, as a segment foundation.

6. Press a red E onto the shiny side of an F-E-F foundation, right side up. Pin an F along one side of E, turn the foundation over and stitch. Turning back to the fabric side, trim the seam to a scant $\frac{1}{4}''$ and press open the pieces. Repeat for the other side of E. Make 16 F-E-F wedges.

7. Press a dark blue strip on the shiny side of a C point, right side up, with the cut edge $\frac{1}{4}''$ over the center line. Pin a medium blue strip on top of the dark blue, right sides together. Stitch from the drawn line side, trim and press as before. Make eight C points. Since you used strips, you will need to trim the seam allowances on all outside edges of the shape to a scant $\frac{1}{4}''$.

8. Press the center fabric on the shiny side of A, and press-piece on the 8 small triangles, B, one to a side. Be careful to stitch only on the drawn line, not catching any seam allowances in the sewing.

9. Press the 8 D points onto the wrong side of brown fabric, leaving space between them. Cut out, $\frac{1}{4}''$ beyond the edge of each foundation.

10. Set four C split points in between the B triangles in the north-south-east-west positions of the Compass (Figure 6-21). Match the cut edges of the pieces and use the freezer paper as stitching guides. This forms the outline of the Compass star.

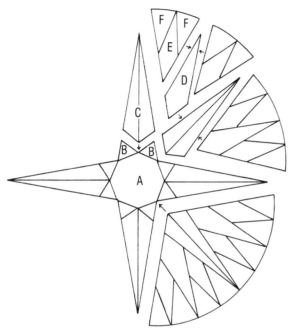

Figure 6-21. Construction progression.

11. Sew F-E-F wedges to each side of the D points.

12. Sew F-E-F-D-F-E-F wedges to each side of the remaining C points.

13. Set the large wedges thus formed into the angles between the remaining B-C points. This completes the Mariner's Compass center.

It is important to sew only one seam at a time, using the foundations as stitching lines, and not catching any seam allowances in cross seams. By sewing and pressing on the freezer paper, the measurements will remain true, and the edges of the points and wedges will fit exactly (Figure 6-22).

Figure 6-22. Reverse side of Mariner's Compass block, with foundations in place.

14. Fold the piece of background fabric on which you drew the large circle in half, quarters and eighths. Mark these positions on the outline of the circle to provide matching points for setting the Compass into the block. Cut out the circle (Figure 6-20), being careful not to stretch the edge. Pin the pieced Compass into this circle, matching the major points to the marks and the edges of the freezer paper wedges to the drawn line of the circle. Stitch from the Compass side, so that you don't cut off any points inadvertently. The Mariner's Compass can also be inserted into the circle by appliqué, by reverse appliqué, or by using Caryl Fallert's English machine piecing technique. (See Chapter 3.)

15. Create an inner border for the block with Uzbek arrowheads (see Chapter 8), or if you prefer a plain inner border, cut four $1\frac{1}{2}'' \times 14''$ strips from one of the fabrics from the quilt and four $1\frac{1}{2}''$ squares of a contrasting fabric for cornerstones. Attach to the quilt top. For the outer border, with either inner border, cut four $3\frac{1}{2}'' \times 22''$ strips. Stitch onto each side, mitering the corners. (See Chapter 8.) Once the borders are on, remove the papers.

16. Baste, quilt, and bind with background fabric. Points of the Compass were outline quilted, and radiating lines in the points were extended into the background. The outer border was quilted with curved lines, in a cable variation.

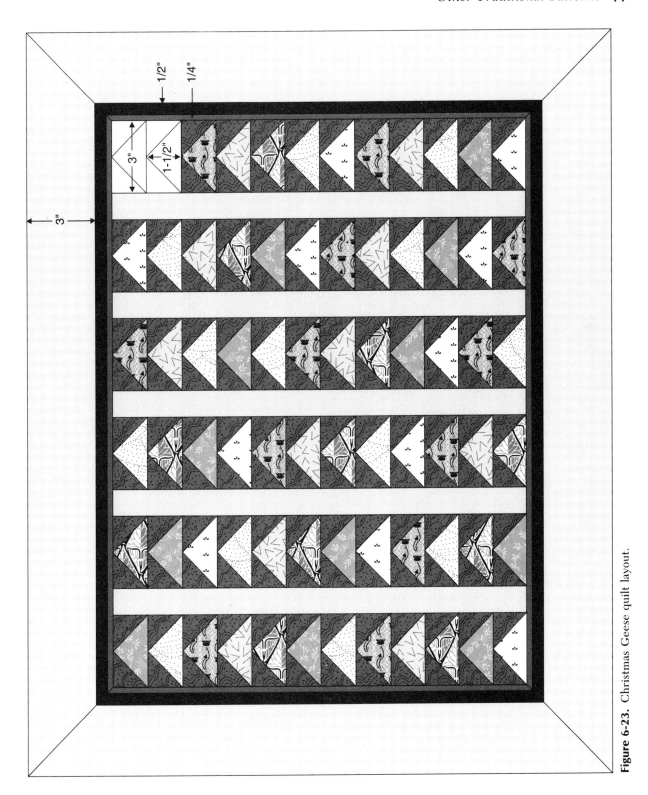

Figure 6-23. Christmas Geese quilt layout.

Christmas Geese
by Jane Hall
(Color Plate 33)

Flying Geese is one of the most popular patterns in a quilter's repertoire. It is a pleasing design, allowing for contrasts and play of color. It is versatile, and can be used as the pattern in a body of a quilt, as an accent, or as a border. It is a pattern that is sometimes difficult to execute accurately because of the number of pieces and the need to keep the points of the triangles uniformly accurate.

Our project uses the arrangement known as Flying Geese Bars, with bars of triangles separated by vertical strips of plain fabric (Figure 6-23). We used *under* foundation pressed-piecing on tracing paper for the Geese bars, and freezer paper single foundations for the joining strips, to assure stability and accuracy.

Quilt Size: 32″ × 26″

Block Size: 3″ × 18″ strip (6 strips)

Materials

Assortment of 10–12 light and medium greens, prints or solids

$\frac{1}{4}$ yd of one of the greens for setting bars (also used for some of the geese)

$\frac{1}{2}$ yd of one of the greens for the outer border (also used for some of the geese)

8–10 $2\frac{1}{2}$ inch strips of the remaining greens, cut across the fabric

$\frac{1}{2}$ yd background fabric, dark contrasting print

$\frac{1}{8}$ yd of dark green and bright red solid fabrics for inner borders

Backing fabric; batting; binding

Tracing paper; freezer paper

Construction Directions

1. Trace the Flying Geese pattern onto tracing paper (Figure 6-24). There are twelve geese in one bar. It is fast and accurate to draw all six bars at one time on a large sheet of tracing paper, by extending the cross-lines. Separate the foundation bars before sewing onto them.

2. On the dull side of freezer paper, draw 5 setting strips, each $1\frac{1}{4}″ × 18″$. Mark off twelve increments of $1\frac{1}{2}″$ each. Again, it is accurate to do these in groups, extending the cross-lines.

3. Cut out the freezer paper strips and iron each piece onto the back of the fabric you have chosen for the setting strips, leaving at least $\frac{1}{2}″$ between them. Cut out the fabric, using a rotary cutter and ruler to measure a $\frac{1}{4}″$ seam allowance outside the edge of the freezer paper foundation.

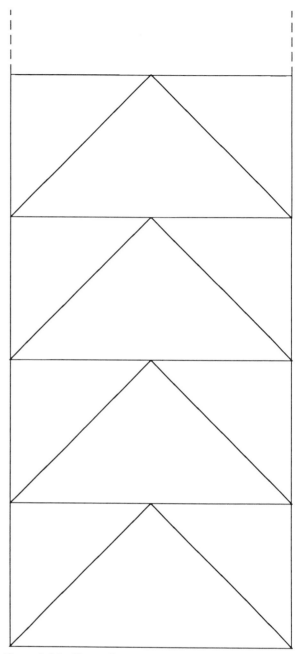

Figure 6-24. Flying Geese pattern.

4. Cut a $2\frac{1}{2}″$ strip from each of the green fabrics, including that used for the setting strips and the border. Using a plastic square, cut all the green strips of fabric into right-angle triangles, placing the square on the strips so that the right angle is at one side of the strip, and the long side of the triangle is along the opposite side of the strip (Figure 6-25). You will need a total of 72 green triangles for the geese.

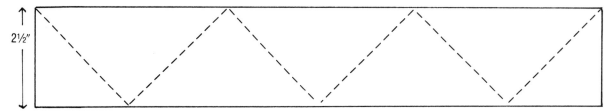

Figure 6-25. Cutting diagram for green triangles.

5. Cut five strips of background fabric, $2\frac{3}{4}''$ wide, across the width of the fabric. Cut these strips into squares, and cut the squares on the diagonal to make the setting triangles for each side of the green triangles.

6. Arrange the triangles in a pleasing color gradation, over six bars. We used dark to light, suggesting a V formation. It would be equally effective with random placement of colors.

7. Place the first green triangle of strip #1 on the undrawn side of the tracing paper foundation, right side up. Lay one of the background triangles along one side edge of the triangle, right sides together, and pin in place. Be sure that the pattern lines are covered by the pieces, with adequate seam allowances. This is easily checked with tracing paper, which is translucent. Turn the foundation over, and stitch on the line, from two stitches before it begins to two stitches after it ends.

8. Turn back to the fabric side of the foundation, trim the excess fabric, open the strip and pin in place. Repeat for the second background triangle. Pressing at the completion of each rectangle helps keep the strip flat.

9. Lay the second green triangle along the edges of the first rectangle just completed, right side down. Pin in place, turn the foundation over, and stitch as before. Continue piecing the triangles to complete six bars.

10. Pin the setting strips, with freezer paper on them, to the Flying Geese bars, matching the drawn marks on the freezer paper with the bottom lines of the triangles (Figure 6-26). Stitch, using the paper edges as sewing guides.

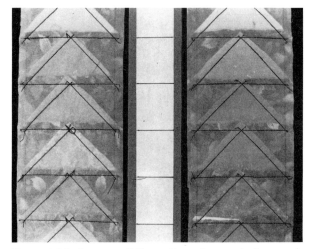

Figure 6-26. Reverse of Flying Geese bars with the setting strip ready to sew together.

11. Cut the border fabric as follows:
   red: two strips $\frac{3}{4}'' \times 21''$; two strips $\frac{3}{4}'' \times 27''$
   dark green: two strips $1'' \times 22''$; two strips $1'' \times 28''$
   medium green: two strips $3\frac{1}{2}'' \times 30''$; two strips $3\frac{1}{2}'' \times 35''$

Add the borders to the quilt top one at a time, mitering the corners separately. (See Chapter 8.) It is much easier to sew a narrow enclosed border straight if you gauge your stitching line by the previous line of stitching rather than by the cut edges.

12. At this point, remove all the papers from geese strips and from the setting bars.

13. Baste, quilt and bind with the outer border fabric. We quilted to emphasize the Flying Geese, outlining and quilting with angled lines within each green triangle. The setting strips and inner borders were outlined "in the ditch." The outer border was quilted with overlapping half-circles.

Plate 17. Antique *Pineapple Log Cabin*. Maker unknown, circa 1895. 62″ × 72″. From the collection of Jane Hall.

Plate 18. Antique *Courthouse Steps Log Cabin*. Maker unknown, circa 1890. 75″ × 80″. From the collection of Jane Hall.

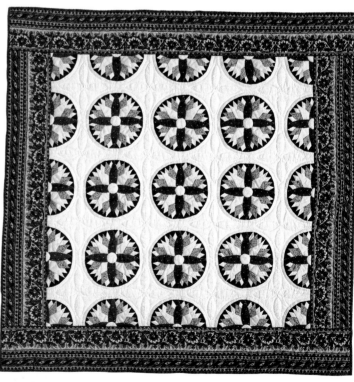

Plate 19. *Oak and Sumac.* Dixie Haywood, 1991. 84″ × 110″.

Plate 20. *Mariner's Compass* Variation. Joann Wilson, Pensacola, Florida, 1991. 28″ × 28″.

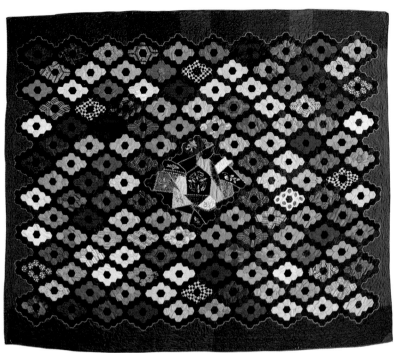

Plate 21. Antique silk *Honeycomb Mosaic.* Maker unknown, made in Buncombe County, N.C., circa 1860. 76″ × 84″. From the collection of Aly Goodwin: The N.E. Horton Antique Quilt Collection, Black Mountain, N.C.

Plate 22. *When Grandmother's Lilies Bloomed.* Eileen Sullivan, Columbia, S.C., 1990. 63″ × 84″. Photo courtesy of the American Quilter's Society, Paducah, Ky.

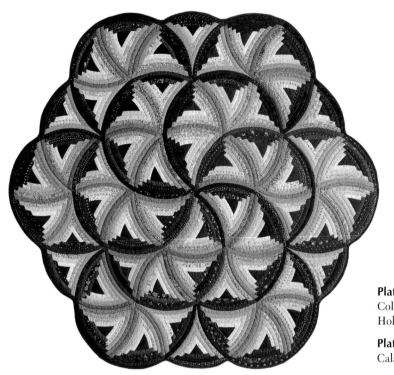

Plate 23. *Fantasy Too.* June Ryker, Lakewood, Colo., 1990. 47″ diameter. Quilted by Linda Holtz, Wheatland, Wyo.

Plate 24. *Equus Equinox.* Cheryl Trostrud-White, Calabasas, Calif., 1990. 85″ × 98″.

Plate 25. *Ring Around the Roses.* Jennifer Amor, Columbia, S.C., 1984. 22″ × 22″.

Plate 26. *Long May She Wave.* Dory Sandon, North Palm Beach, Florida, 1990. 44″ × 54″. Photo from *Discover America and Friends Sharing America,* Dutton Studio Press and the Museum of American Folk Art, New York, 1991.

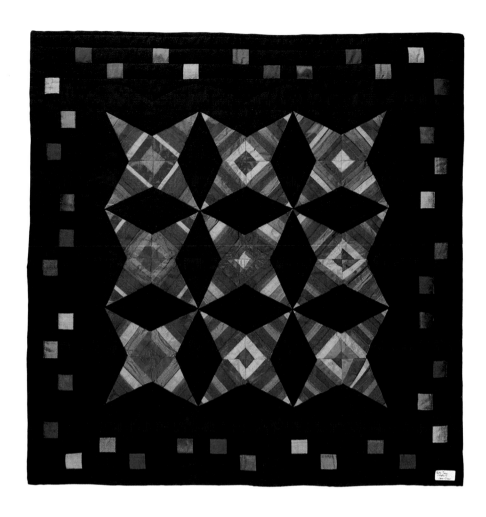

Plate 27. *Party Time* by Jane Hall and Dixie Haywood.

Plate 28. *Chromania Too* by Dixie Haywood.

Plate 29. *White Collar* quilt by Mary Golden.

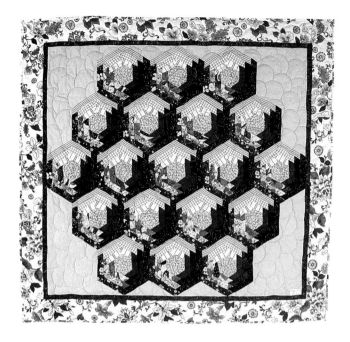

Plate 30. *Blueberries and Cream* by Janet Elwin.

Plate 31. *Spinners* by Jane Hall.

Plate 32. *Mariner's Compass* with Uzbek border by Jane Hall.

Plate 33. *Christmas Geese* by Jane Hall.

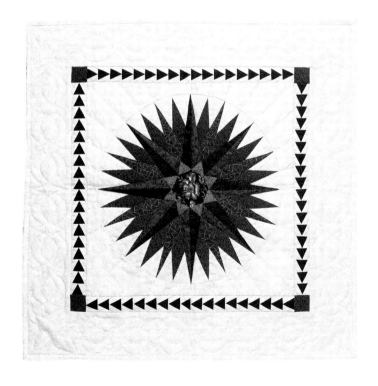

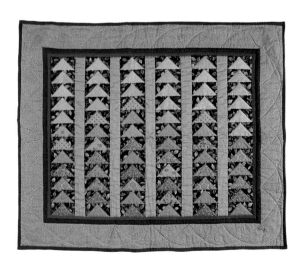

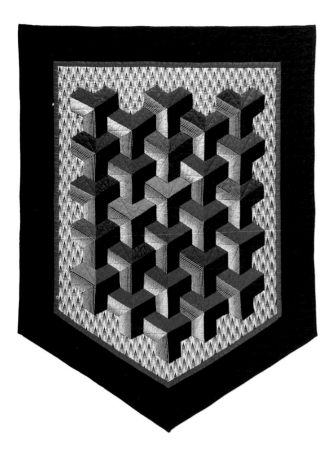

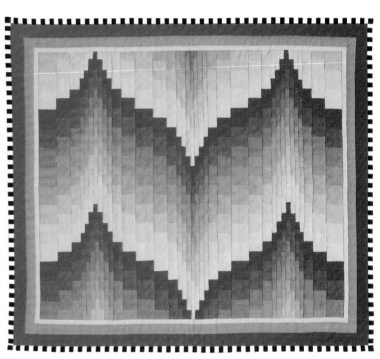

Plate 34. *Highrise* by Dixie Haywood.

Plate 35. *Flamingo Flambé* by Jennifer Amor.

Plate 36. *Peace Lily* by Eileen Sullivan.

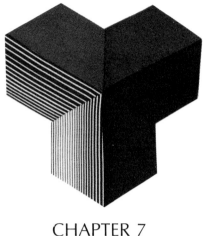

CHAPTER 7

Single Foundation Piecing

Single foundation piecing is a non-pressed piecing technique involving a single paper template for each piece in the block. The foundation is, in effect, a template and is affixed to the piece of fabric temporarily. It is used as a guide for assembling the pieces and serves the same purpose as a pressed pieced foundation: stabilizing and providing precision in piecing.

The traditional example of single foundation piecing is English template piecing (Figure 7-1). In this technique, the fabric for each piece is basted over an individual foundation which has been cut to the exact size of the finished patch. The edges of two prepared patches are aligned, right sides facing, and are joined with whipstitching. The precision results from matching finished edges and points (Figure 7-2). A variety of patterns have been made with this technique, often consisting of only one shape. Common shapes used have been triangles, diamonds, clamshells and, most familiar, hexagons. Color Plate 21 shows a beautiful antique silk Hexagon Mosaic quilt with an unusual Crazy Quilt motif in the center. Conversely, Figure 7-3 illustrates the

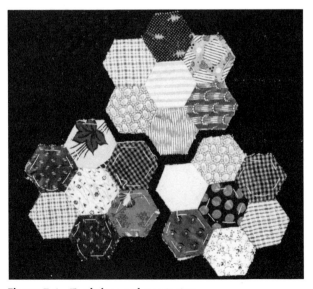

Figure 7-1. English template piecing.

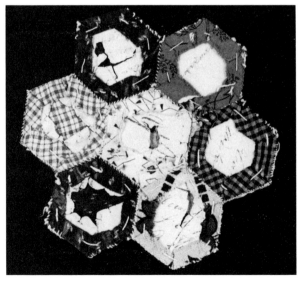

Figure 7-2. Back of English template pieced section.

Figure 7-3. Center detail of Antique Crazy Quilt in Color Plate 7.

use of English pieced hexagons as a major design element in the center of a Victorian Crazy quilt block.

A more contemporary use of single foundation piecing involves cutting foundations from paper and attaching them, temporarily, to fabric pieces. Ordinary paper, including tracing paper, is generally affixed with a glue stick; freezer paper can simply be pressed onto the fabric. The foundations serve as a basis for cutting pieces with a $\frac{1}{4}''$ seam allowance. The pieces are joined seam-to-seam using the edges of the foundations as guides. This method retains the precision of the historic technique while eliminating the tedium of basting and whip-stitching (Figure 7-4).

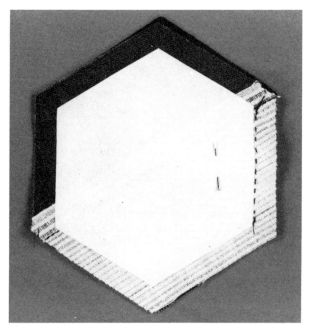

Figure 7-4. Single foundation with seam-to-seam piecing.

This is the only technique using a removable foundation that is easily worked by hand. It gives a highly visible sewing line for either hand or machine sewing and is akin to the pencil line often used for hand-piecing. Drawing on some fabrics is difficult due to their color or texture; it is also more repetitive than gluing or pressing paper foundations to the wrong sides of the fabric.

You may have more than one option for piecing a given pattern. As we said in the previous chapter, when adapting pressed-piecing to a complex pattern, it is often necessary to divide the piecing into segments, using pressed-piecing for some, and single foundation piecing or seam-to-seam piecing for others. In the same vein, when using single foundation piecing, there may be parts of the pattern that could be press-pieced easily, saving time and providing precision.

All sorts of complex traditional patterns, pictorial scenes, and designs from other media can be used with single foundation piecing. For instance, a landscape can be pieced with the single foundation format, following the lines inherent in the picture. Or, in a technique explored by Georgia Bonesteel, the picture can be grid-ruled in one direction and transferred to a freezer paper foundation (Georgia Bonesteel, *New Ideas for Lap Quilting* [Birmingham: Oxmoor House, 1987] 62–77). After the paper is cut apart and pressed onto appropriate fabric, the pieces are sewn into strips matching the grids. These are joined easily by machine to complete the picture. With both methods, the foundations need to be numbered to avoid confusion during construction.

With a pattern where each piece is a different shape, such as our Getting Started block, making a template for each piece and tracing it onto fabric would take much more time than using single foundation piecing. The fabric pieces prepared with these foundations can then be joined with ease and accuracy.

Equus Equinox, (Color Plate 24), by Cheryl Trostrud-White, is composed of two different horse blocks which were constructed entirely using single template piecing with freezer paper. To avoid image reversal, she traced her design on tracing paper. Then she turned the paper over and transferred the design to freezer paper. Several layers of freezer paper were cut at the same time, with each piece labeled as it was cut.

She planned her color placement by value, to evoke images of a trotting horse seen in half-day, half-night, during the summer equinox. She selected her fabrics for sky-horse-ground in each block within that scheme. She pressed the freezer paper templates to the wrong side of the appropriate fabric, "eyeballed" the seam allowance, and stitched the pieces together using seam-to-seam piecing.

Freezer paper foundations have another advantage over traditional templates in this type of piecing. There is no chance that a foundation piece will be flipped or cut absent-mindedly on the wrong side of the fabric, either of which would reverse the piece and make it unusable.

■ Getting Started ■

Armadillo Block
(Figure 7-5)

Figure 7-5. Armadillo block. From *Creature Comforts*, by Marie Shirer and Barbara Brackman (Wallace-Homestead, 1986). Designed by Marie Shirer.

This delightful creature provides a chance to try out single foundation piecing in a block where every shape is different. Our sample took less than three hours to make, pieced by machine. It is adapted from *Creature Comforts* by Marie Shirer and Barbara Brackman (Wallace-Homestead, 1986).

1. Enlarge the diagram (Figure 7-6) to the desired size to create a master block. We used a copy machine to arrive at a $12\frac{7}{8}''$ block, by progressively enlarging copies 133% once and 155% twice. For the second 155% enlargement, it was necessary to copy half the design at a time. Because copies were recopied, we had to square up the block by extending the top about $\frac{1}{8}''$. This slight distortion did not affect the pictorial design noticeably.

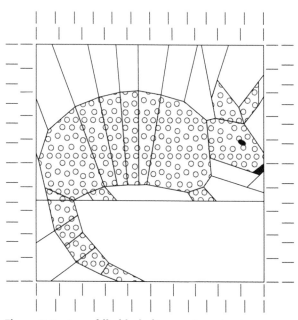

Figure 7-6. Armadillo block diagram for enlarging.

The guidelines around the block can be used to enlarge the block by the grid method. The smaller marks will divide the design into ten grids; the larger marks are for a twelve grid division. If the design is transferred to a sheet with twelve one inch square grids, the block will be twelve inches. If the twelve grids are $1\frac{1}{2}''$ square, the resulting block will measure 18".

2. Trace the design onto the dull side of a sheet of freezer paper. The design will be reversed; if this is not desired, trace the design on the shiny side of the paper. Number each section as indicated in Figure 7-7, and cut the pattern apart.

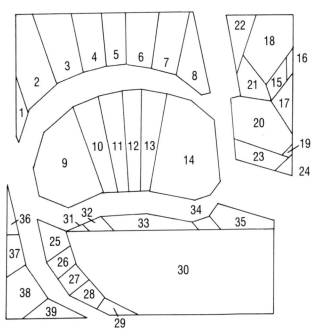

Figure 7-7. Numbered piecing order for Armadillo block.

3. Iron each foundation to the wrong side of the appropriate fabric, leaving at least ½″ space between them. Cut out the pieces, adding ¼″ seam allowance around all edges. It is fast, easy, and accurate to do this with a rotary cutter.

4. Lay the pieces, with the foundations up, on the master block, to keep them in order. Piece into sections following Figure 7-7. Use the edge of the foundations as a sewing guide and the numbers as the sewing order. For instance, the head section is started by piecing #15 and #16, then adding #17 and #18. Piece #19, #20 and #21 together and connect them to the 15–18 section, with #22, #23, and #24 added in sequence. When the sections are complete, sew them together. Remove the freezer paper and press.

High Rise
by Dixie Haywood
(Color Plate 34)

High Rise uses single foundation piecing with freezer paper for an Inner City adaptation (Figure 7-8). The pattern unit is constructed of pairs of trapezoids which form hexagons. It could have been pieced from individual trapezoids using traditional English template piecing. This project introduces a quick piecing method combined with single foundation piecing.

Quilt Size: 27″ × 35″

Materials
Combinations totaling approximately ¾ yd of assorted red and purple solid fabrics
1 yd black fabric
1 yd black and white striped fabric
1⅛ yd background fabric, print or contrasting solid
Backing fabric; batting; binding
Freezer paper; small piece of template plastic

Construction Directions
1. Cut nine widths each of the stripe, solid black and the red/purple fabrics, all 2″ wide. Cut each strip in half, resulting in pieces approximately 22″ long.

2. Stitch pairs of strips together lengthwise in the following sets: black and stripe (A), black and red (B), red and stripe (C). Press the seams towards the darker side (Figure 7-9).

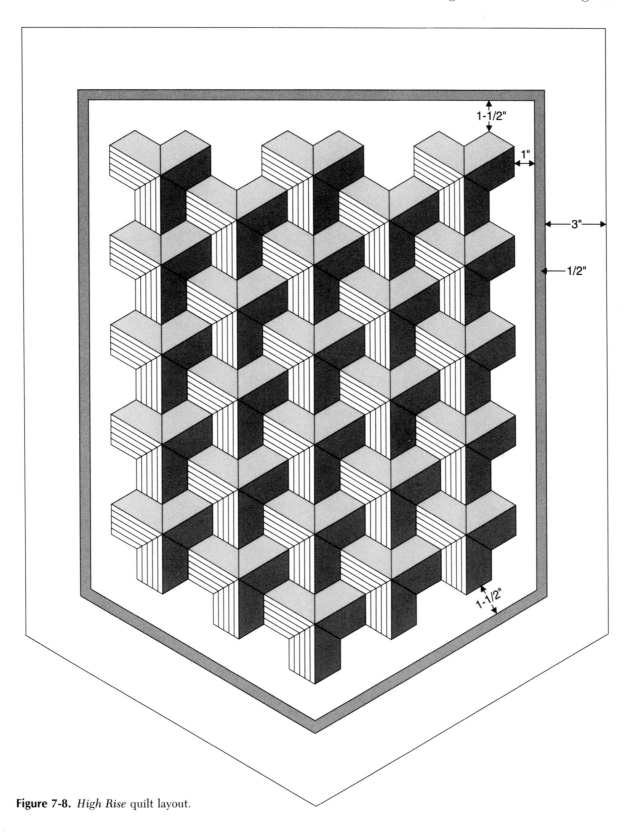

Figure 7-8. *High Rise* quilt layout.

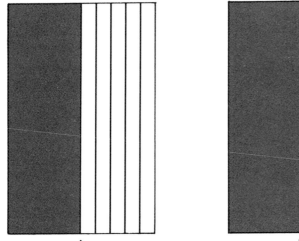
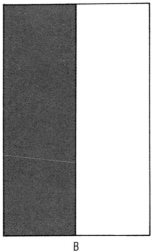
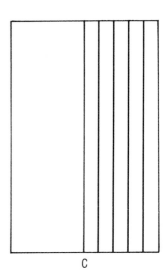

A   B   C

Figure 7-9. Three types of strip panels.

3. Make a plastic template from Pattern A (Figure 7-10). Cut 90 foundations from freezer paper. To do this quickly, trace 18 hexagons on freezer paper. Fold the paper to make five layers, staple or pin the layers together in the center of each hexagon, and cut out. Remove staples. (This will give you four extra design units so you will have some options when laying out the design.)

4. Lay the foundations on the wrong side of the strip panels, shiny side against the fabric. Line up opposite points of each freezer paper foundation on the seam line of the panels. Leave $\frac{5}{8}''$ spaces between the foundations for seam allowance (Figure 7-11). Cut 30 hexagons from each group of panels, A, B, and C. Use a rotary cutter or scissors, and leave a $\frac{1}{4}''$ seam allowance around each hexagon.

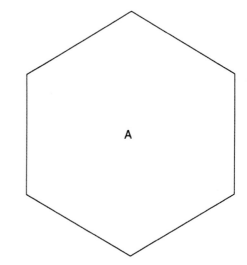

Figure 7-10. Template for piece A.

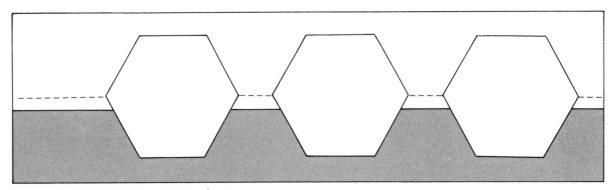

Figure 7-11. Freezer paper foundations laid on panel.

Note: Because of the bending each hexagon receives as the top is pieced, the freezer paper may loosen. It can be re-ironed or pinned in place. Even better is to quickly machine baste from point to point across the templates with a long stitch (Figure 7-12).

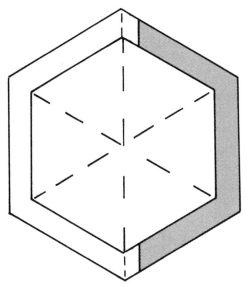

Figure 7-12. Freezer paper foundation basted onto fabric piece.

5. A unit is formed by matching the colors of each panel (Figure 7-13). Lay out the design on the background fabric, arranging the colors into a

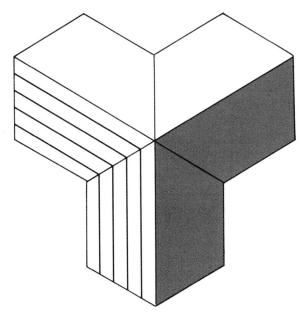

Figure 7-13. *High Rise* unit.

balanced composition. When you are satisfied with the arrangement, pin each hexagon to the fabric to retain the design as you piece the units.

6. Piece a unit of the design at a time, by matching colors, lining up the cut edges of each hexagon, and checking that the edges of the foundations are aligned. Stitch together from the center seam outward (Figure 7-14). These units are as easily pieced by hand as by machine. Do not stitch into the seam allowances of the hexagons. Re-pin each unit to the layout as it is pieced.

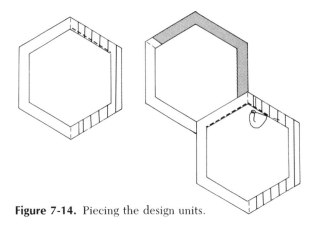

Figure 7-14. Piecing the design units.

7. Join the units in vertical rows, and then join the rows. When the design is complete, wrap the seam allowances over the foundations at the outside edges of the design, and baste.

8. Position the design on the background fabric 2″ from the edges of the background, and appliqué in place. Cut out the background fabric from beneath the design. Remove the basting and the foundations and press carefully. Trim the background fabric to $1\frac{1}{4}''$ at each side and $1\frac{3}{4}''$ at the top and bottom.

9. Cut three widths of red fabric 1″ wide and 3 widths of black fabric 3½″ wide for the border. Sew the red border first to the sides, next to the top, and then to the bottom edges. Miter the two upper corners at a 45 degree angle and the three bottom corners at a 60 degree angle. Repeat with the black border.

10. Baste, quilt, and bind with black fabric. The Inner City units were quilted from point to point through the centers (Figure 7-15). The background was quilted on the pattern of the fabric. The border was quilted in equilateral triangles.

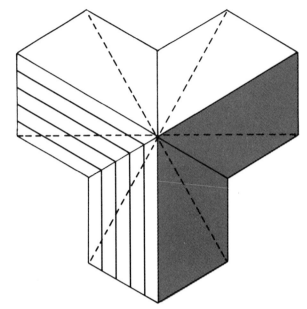

Figure 7-15. *High Rise* unit quilting design.

CHAPTER 8

Borders and Strips on Foundation

Pieced borders and strips are wonderful additions to quilts. They often are not attempted because it can be difficult to achieve a precise fit. An accurately pieced border can "grow" even with a straight-grain edge. (When we refer to borders in this chapter, we also mean to include strips; in the interests of brevity we omit the word.)

Some of the most effective pieced borders are those made with simple repeated shapes such as checkerboards, squares-on-point, sawtooth, and Flying Geese (Figure 8-1). When these small squares or triangles are pieced together in a long strip, they are prone to stretch beyond the original dimension. String borders, often done on a diagonal, are even more difficult to keep flat and accurate (Figure 8-2).

Piecing these borders on foundations can alleviate most stretch problems and produce borders which will fit the quilts, as well as add visual excitement. Since the prime reason for using foundations for borders is to control stretch, we believe temporary foundations are the best choice for border foundations because of their firmness.

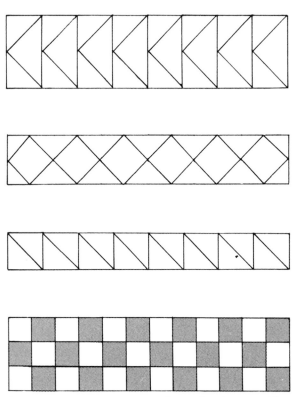

Figure 8-1. Common geometric shapes found in pieced borders.

Figure 8-2. Antique wool Log Cabin quilt top with diagonal borders, pieced on foundations.

When measuring for a border on any quilt, care must be taken to measure the quilt top at a stabilized section, such as along a seam that joins blocks. When the blocks of a quilt are foundation pieced, it is easy to measure the dimensions of the quilt top for a border before the foundations are removed. Even if the foundations in the center of the quilt have been removed for easier handling, the foundations along the edge should remain in place until any borders are attached to avoid the stretch inherent in any unquilted top.

The pieced pattern you chose for the border unit must fit into both the crosswise and lengthwise borders, with the corners treated consistently. It is possible to add another element, such as a plain section at corners, between units, or in mid-length to achieve this fit.

In addition to measuring the length of the borders, to plan a pieced border effectively you need to consider the size of the block and the size of the border unit. If your quilt includes strips or interior plain borders, these measurements will, of course, have to be taken into consideration. They can be helpful in balancing measurements of the border units and blocks. Sometimes these measurements will mesh exactly. More often one, usually the border unit, takes precedence.

For instance, if you have five 12″ blocks, and want to add a Flying Geese border with $1\frac{1}{2}$″ units, eight border units will fit each block without an adjustment (Figure 8-3). If your border unit is $2\frac{1}{2}$″ wide, it will not match at each block seam, but will fit the quilt, with a complete border unit at the center of the quilt (Figure 8-4). Either of these scenarios is workable.

Once you have worked out the fit of the border, you need to decide how to mark and

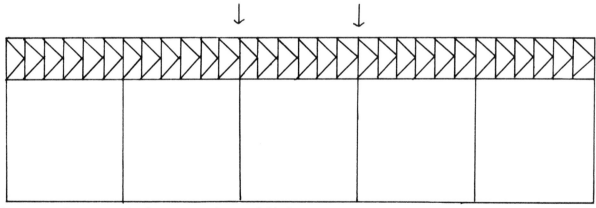

Figure 8-3. Flying Geese border units matching each block.

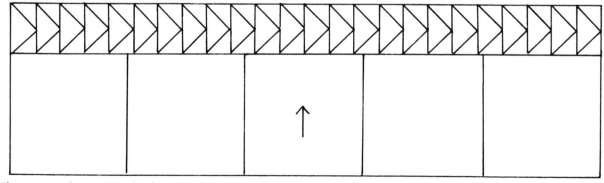

Figure 8-4. Flying Geese border units fitting length of border, but not matching each block.

piece the border foundation. Some patterns such as Flying Geese, can be pieced directly onto the foundation, which would be marked with piecing lines. Other patterns, such as checkerboard, or a square-on-point, must be partially pre-pieced, often by quick-piecing techniques, before they are press-pieced onto the foundation. This foundation needs to be marked with unit placement lines (Figure 8-5). Either *top* or *under* pressed-piecing can be used.

A sawtooth border can be foundation pieced in either way. If only two fabrics are used, it makes sense to quick piece half square triangles and sew the completed squares to the foundation. If you are piecing a scrap border, it would be easier to press-piece each individual triangle to the foundation. Whatever your choice, there are no shortcuts to accuracy. Both quick-pieced units and individual pieces must fit the foundation markings.

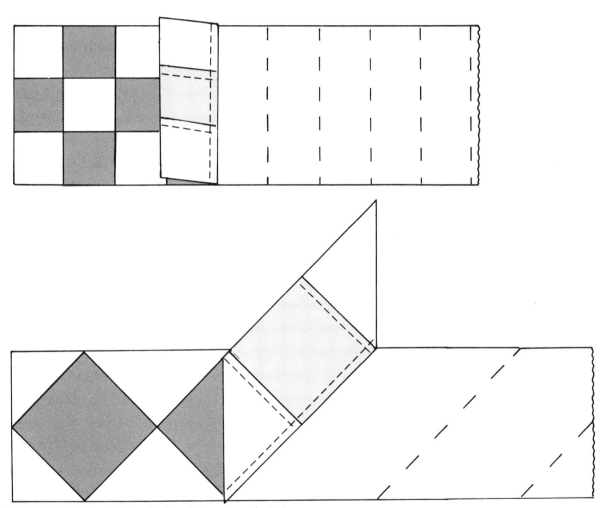

Figure 8-5. Pre-pieced units for foundation pressed-piecing.

The foundation can be made the entire length of the border or divided into manageable pieces for easier handling and sewing. If you choose to work with smaller sections you can break the foundation with the assurance that it will fit back together perfectly.

Dawn's Early Light (Color Plate 11) illustrates several of the advantages of piecing borders on a foundation. Since Dixie wanted the border colors to coordinate with color changes in the quilt, she needed to make individual border foundations to match each outer block in the quilt top (Figure 8-6). Each border foundation was pieced to fit into the color gradations of the quilt.

Figure 8-6. Reverse of *Dawn's Early Light* quilt top, showing border units with matching blocks.

The angle of the strips put the edges of the border on the bias. This would have been a nightmare to fit without the stabilization provided by the foundation. To add even more stability to the bias edges, the sections of the border were stay-stitched a scant $\frac{1}{4}''$ from the long edges of the foundation after each was completed. The foundation remained in place until the final one-fabric border was added, making that border easy to measure and attach.

Another advantage of piecing a border on a foundation is that adjustments in fit can be made with confidence. Dixie wanted to use strips that had been cut for the blocks, but did not fit the length of the border sections exactly. Rather than recut the strips to an odd fraction, it was a simple matter to adjust the seam allowance slightly on two or three strips, so that the strips fit the guide provided by the foundation.

For many designs, a mitered border is the classic finishing touch. There are numerous methods for mitering a corner by using rulers, folding the border fabric, or pressing the miter angle. The bias stretch of the fabric as it is cut and stitched along the 45 degree angle can cause ripples and inaccurate corners. The firmness of a foundation is invaluable when mitering corners on both pieced and unpieced borders.

To make a perfect miter, cut four pieces of freezer paper each measuring the width of the border by two times the width of the border. Cut at a 45 degree angle near the center, cutting two pieces of freezer paper in one direction and the remaining two in the opposite direction. On the dull side of the freezer paper, draw $\frac{1}{4}''$ seam allowances along the angle and the short edge (Figure 8-7). Iron a freezer paper angle to each end of a measured fabric border, with the intersection of the drawn lines placed at the finished inside measurement of the quilt (which is also the finished edge measurement of the border).

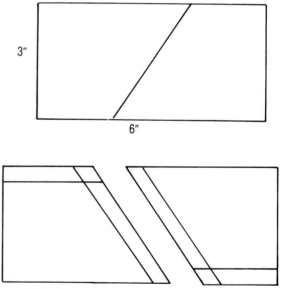

Figure 8-7. Cutting and marking freezer paper for mitered corners.

Sew the border to the quilt, starting and stopping the stitching at the intersection of the lines (Figure 8-8). Repeat on the remaining sides. When all the borders are in place, fold the quilt top so that you can match the cut edges and the lines on the freezer paper for two adjacent corners. Stitch the angle on the drawn line, starting

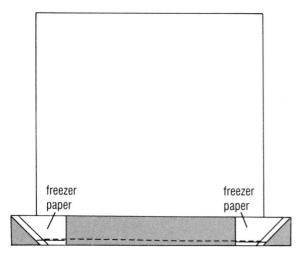

Figure 8-8. Sewing a prepared border to quilt top.

at the intersection (Figure 8-9). Do not stitch across the seam allowances. Trim off excess fabric and remove the foundations.

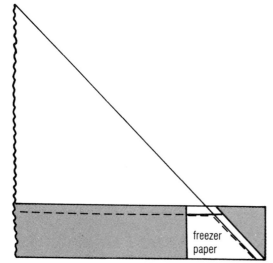

Figure 8-9. Sewing the miter.

■ Getting Started ■

Uzbek Arrowheads
by Jane Hall
(Figure 8-10)

In addition to the types of pieced borders discussed in general in this chapter, we refer you to instructions for the pieced border on the *Party*

Figure 8-10. Uzbek arrowheads used as border.

Time quilt in Chapter 3, and on the *Chromania Too* quilt in Chapter 4.

The hand-sewn designs known as Koraki, from central Asia, are filled with familiar shapes and patterns. The triangle is the sign for holy protection and is put into patterns that we would call Flying Geese. Yvonne Porcella has used one type of triangle pattern from this region very effectively in clothing. (Karen Kinney Drellich, *Yvonne Porcella: Nurse turned Fabric Designer*. [Peoria, IL: PJS Publications, Inc., Sew News, No. 30, March 1985] 62–63.) It works equally well in quilts.

We have adapted these tiny triangular shapes which resemble arrowheads for borders around the *Mariner's Compass* quilt (Color Plate 32), a Chapter 6 Getting Started project. They could also be used for strips, or for accents within a quilt. We used *under* foundation pressed-piecing on tracing paper.

Border Strip Size: $1'' \times 13\frac{1}{2}''$, constructed from $\frac{3}{4}''$ equilateral triangles with $\frac{1}{8}''$ background on each side.

Materials
$\frac{1}{8}$ yd dark color fabric for arrowheads
$\frac{1}{4}$ yd light color fabric for background
Tracing paper

Construction Directions
1. Cut four pieces of good quality tracing paper, each $2'' \times 16''$. Trace the pattern (Figure 8-11) on two of the papers, extending it to measure $13\frac{1}{2}''$ (18 arrowheads). Repeat on the remaining two papers, adding a $1\frac{1}{2}''$ square at each end.

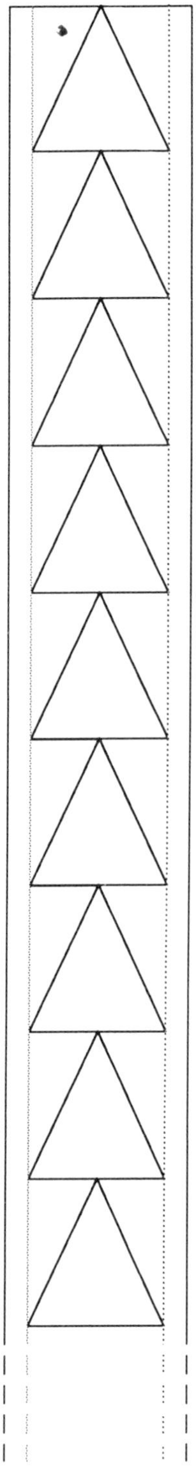

Figure 8-11. Pattern for Uzbek arrowheads.

3. Pin a dark square of fabric on the undrawn side of the foundation, wrong side of the fabric against the paper. Turn the foundation over and trim the edges of the fabric to an angle, following the drawn lines of the triangle as a guide, and including seam allowance.

4. Pin a piece of background fabric onto one side of the dark triangle, right sides together. Turn the foundation over and *under* press-piece, stitching on the line. Trim any excess fabric; press open the strip. Repeat with a strip on the other side of the dark triangle.

It is important to press each unit as you go, because of the amount of fabric and the number of stitches in such a small area. Pull gently on the foundation strip as you press, to keep it to size. Take care not to over-iron the uncovered tracing paper as it may shrink slightly, and will lose flexibility.

5. Lay the second dark square across the first arrowhead, right sides together, making certain that the stitching line is covered with an adequate seam allowance. Stitch, trim the seam, and press up the dark square. Using the cut edge of the previously sewn background strips as a guide, trim off the corners of the square so that you will have an accurate angle for laying on the next background strip (Figure 8-12). Place and sew

Figure 8-12. Trimming the dark fabric to a triangular shape.

2. Cut the dark fabric into four $1\frac{1}{4}''$ strips, across the width of the fabric. Cut $1\frac{1}{4}''$ squares from the strips. Cut the background fabric into six $1''$ strips, across the width of the fabric. Cut these strips into $1\frac{1}{2}''$ lengths.

the two background strips for this triangle, trimming and pressing as before (Figure 8-13).

Figure 8-13. Light strip laid in place for stitching.

6. Continue up the foundation strip, adding background strips to each side of the dark triangles in order.

7. To complete these strips as a border, arrange them with the arrowheads facing in the direction you wish. They can chase around the block or meet at opposite corners. Add 1½" squares to both ends of two border strips to complete the border.

8. These strips can be sewn to the block on the line along the side points of the arrowheads. If you wish to "float" the arrowheads as we did, from the foundation side of the strips, draw a sewing line ⅛ of an inch beyond the finished side points of the arrowheads. Trim the border with a rotary cutter, leaving a ¼" seam allowance beyond this line. Sew the two borders which have no extra squares on first, on opposite sides of the block. Sew the other two borders across the remaining sides.

This design can be expanded with larger triangles, or longer side strips, which would make the background area in the strip wider. The sizes of the triangles can be varied within a strip. The direction of the arrowheads can change in mid-strip. This option would necessitate piecing two strips and joining them, seam-to-seam.

CHAPTER 9

Innovative Quilts on Foundations

As teachers, we often hear students say, "I love to work with fabric and color but I'm not creative so I'll have to find a pattern I like." We believe people are innately creative whether they realize it or not.

Creativity is more a function of knowledge and experience than of genius. Quiltmakers doing innovative work are those who have control of their medium. It is only with familiarity and practice that one gains the knowledge and confidence to go beyond tradition. Very few creative people—quiltmakers or other artists—have sprung full-blown into innovative work without having served their apprenticeship in both basic techniques and design. We believe that piecing on foundations is a part of these basic techniques, and is another tool for the creative quiltmaker.

Innovation in quiltmaking involves seeing with new eyes and breaking away from the ordinary in unexpected ways. Innovation is not determined by the type of quilt being made, but by the thinking and experimentation that goes into it. A tradition-based design can be more innovative than a clone of someone else's art quilt. Innovation is also relative. It can develop almost by accident, as you try something that appeals to you; or it can be a conscious decision to create something of your own. Usually it's somewhere in between.

When quiltmaking is approached with a cookbook mentality (Take $\frac{1}{4}$ yard of X, add $\frac{1}{2}$ yard of Y, follow the piecing diagram . . .) the "What If?" factor is missing. What if I changed the focus of the block? What if I used an unexpected fabric? What if?, What if?—It is the "What If?" question that takes us beyond the familiar.

In order to do so, we have to be willing to risk failure: wasted time, wasted materials, even ridicule. It is certainly safer to work with established patterns, conventional fabrics, and "decorator colors." Results are guaranteed; there are no unpleasant surprises. The problem with having no unpleasant surprises is that there are usually no surprises, period.

When you have mastered the basics, it is time to give yourself permission to play. Begin with a basic design, study it for ways you could make it your own, for ways it could make a different statement or present a different picture.

This process will not automatically give you the result you want. You need to remember that you are experimenting. You will try many different avenues and may fail, partially or totally. On the other hand, you have a chance to create a special piece. It may not be at all what you had imagined in the beginning. It might lead you to explore a particular concept in depth, or to work in a series.

While we sometimes wonder if working in depth isn't another name for getting in a rut, we both find that the more we play with a given design, the more possibilities we see. Sometimes we play in the cloth, sometimes on paper. Either way, it's a form of brain-storming that is fun and that often leads in new directions.

There is an interesting residual effect of such play. Those who have studied creativity in both artistic and scientific fields have a short-hand term for the process: Saturation, incubation, inspiration. That is, you saturate your mind with a problem or a puzzle. Then when you go on to other activities, even sleep, ideas incubate. Finally, in what can seem a flash of inspiration, the puzzle is solved.

Inspiration can take many directions. Quilters working on foundations with floral motifs have taken different innovative approaches in design and techniques. Jennifer Amor's *Ring Around the Roses* (Color Plate 25), traditional in appearance, is pieced with an adaptation of the technique she is presenting in the Getting Started section of this chapter. The problem of using incredibly small strip-pieced sets to create a representational image was made practical by providing a foundation of removable interfacing.

Eileen Sullivan's inspiration for *When Grandmother's Lily Garden Blooms* (Color Plate 22) was a small mound of lilies in her yard. She wanted to capture the movement, light and shadow, and essence of a flower garden. The quilt is based on the traditional hexagon, which is completely disguised by her innovative design. Like her contribution in the Getting Started section, the entire piece is worked on freezer paper foundations with *under* pressed-piecing.

A different mood was created by Caryl Bryer Fallert in *Garden Party* (Color Plate 2 and detail on page 97). This design is based on large free-form organic shapes derived from nature. The dynamics of the design developed from repeating the shapes at various angles, as well as from her use of strong vibrant colors. She worked on a paper foundation, using string piecing segments contrasting with areas of solid fabric.

Foundation work can expand a quiltmaker's potential in other ways. A former hand piecer, Dory Sandon discovered she could machine piece with a greater degree of precision on foundations, as well as increase her output tremendously. Dory's quilt *Long May She Wave* (Color Plate 26), uses string quilting and strip piecing in imaginative combinations. The Mariner's Compass in the Lady's eye is also foundation-pieced. *Dancing Ribbons* (Figure 9-1), is pieced with string and strip techniques, using color and value changes to achieve depth and dimension.

Figure 9-1. *Dancing Ribbons*, by Dory Sandon, Lake Park, Florida, 1989. 48″ × 76″. From the collection of Mr. and Mrs. Burton Carr, Palm Beach.

Dory draws full-size designs on paper and traces them onto the shiny side of freezer paper, to avoid the reversal of her design. She then transfers the design to the dull side of the freezer paper, adding register marks for easy re-assembly once the paper is cut apart for piecing.

In our own work, on or off-foundation, we vary from traditional to innovative uses of the same pattern. Sometimes an idea prompts us: to create borders as part of the pattern rather than adding them to the quilt later; to make a scenic representation using the pattern; to wash color across the quilt, with a basic pattern as a vehicle. Sometimes it is a particular fabric that inspires us: a print that can be cut up and recombined; a color progression of fabric that can be made to glow; a fabric that creates a particular mood.

We draw and doodle. Then we color diagrams. Both of us feel strongly that paste-ups of a design, using the fabrics involved, are ultimately a more satisfactory way to plan than by drawing and coloring only. The color values of fabric change so dramatically when combined with adjacent fabrics that it is almost impossible to predict the final effect without seeing it first in microcosm. A reducing glass is a valuable tool in this process.

Even then, it is often necessary to make changes as the work progresses. We both work with a design wall that allows us to pin up work and make the necessary changes as we go before the piece is sewn together. Occasionally we even need to change parts after the piece is assembled. Final decisions about borders, bindings, and quilting patterns are made by this same combination of study with trial and error.

Most of the antique and all of the contemporary quilts in the gallery are innovative in one way or another. We have discussed them in the appropriate design chapters. Some of the quilts obviously are based on traditional patterns.

Others have diverged completely from the conventional. Study them to see how other quilters have realized their personal vision.

All of the quilts in this book were worked on foundations. They reinforce our belief that foundation work should be part of a quilter's repertoire in order to have the widest range of techniques from which to draw. It is exciting to see foundation work being taken so far beyond its prosaic origins.

All of us need to give ourselves permission to try new ideas. It is in this spirit that the Getting Started projects are presented. They are a means for you to try adding foundation work to your range of experience, but not to keep you from exploring your own variations. Getting started is necessary for any journey, but it shouldn't be confused with arriving at the destination. That depends on your itinerary, and your own personal vision.

■ Getting Started ■

Flamingo Flambé
by Jennifer Amor
(Color Plate 35)

Bargello is a traditional needlepoint design that can be used to make graphic quilts. Many needlepoint graphs will translate easily into fabric strips, using quick piecing methods. This design requires cutting and sewing with maximum accuracy. A foundation of freezer paper keeps the design accurate and the narrow pieces perfectly straight (Figure 9-2). Both *top* and *under* pressed-piecing are used.

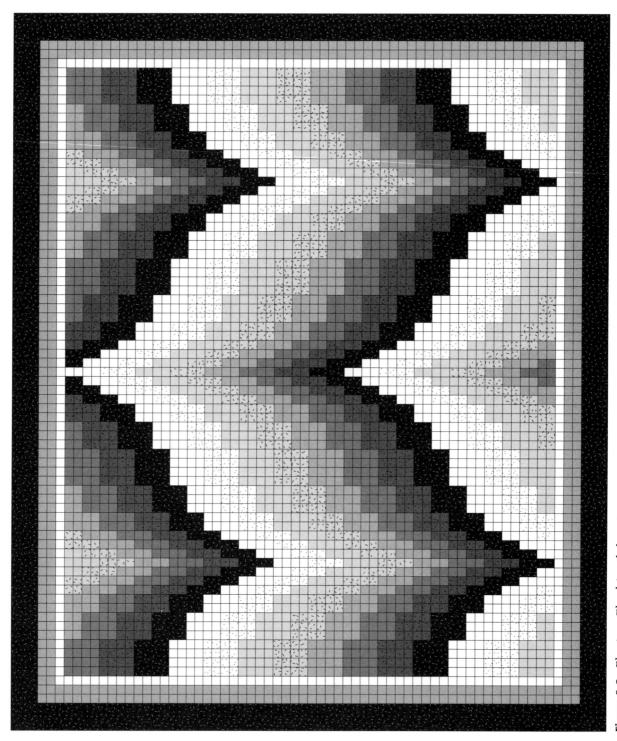

Figure 9-2. *Flamingo Flambé* quilt layout.

Quilt Size: 20″ × 17″

Materials

$\frac{1}{4}$ yd each of 8 shades of one color, from light to dark; fabric should be all the same weight 100% cotton, solids or very small overall prints

$\frac{3}{4}$ yd fabric for quilt back and binding

Quilting ruler with vertical and horizontal grids

Graph paper (at least 10 squares per inch) and colored pencils

Freezer paper

Binding

Construction Directions

Before you begin, take a close look at the bargello pattern. Find the center strip in the design and notice that the pattern is a mirror image: each side of the center strip is identical. Starting with the center strip, you will add 18 more strips of various widths to the left and right sides to complete the design (Figure 9-3).

In making a simple bargello pattern, all the original strips are cut the same size. The resulting strip panel is cut into slices of various widths, and these slices are moved either up or down half a color to achieve the design.

1. Make a chart to follow, using graph paper and colored pencils. To avoid confusion, assign a color code to your fabrics, from light to darkest (A–H), and tape small snips of the fabrics to the edge of your chart, in order.

2. To prepare for strip cutting, rip each fabric on the cross grain, selvage to selvage, and fold in half, matching the torn edges. Don't worry if the two selvages aren't even. Iron a crease at the fold. Fold the fabric again, matching the torn edges and iron a crease at that fold. The fabric is now in four layers, and can be cut evenly with a rotary cutter.

3. Line up the right angle of your ruler with the four-folded edge of the fabric and trim off the torn edges. Cut two $1\frac{1}{2}″$ wide strips from each of the eight colors. Place the cut strips in order, lightest to darkest.

4. Using matching thread and a smaller than usual stitch length, stitch the lightest strip (A) to the next lightest (B), with a $\frac{1}{4}″$ seam allowance. Press the seam towards the darker strip, working from the right side of the fabric to make sure that both strips are fully opened, with no pleats or tucks in the seam. Use the side of your iron rather than the point, to avoid curving the seam. Press with steam or a damp pressing cloth to get a flat seam.

5. Add the next strip in the color progression (C), this time sewing in the opposite direction. Each time you add a strip, change the sewing direction to keep your panel from curving. Keep one end of the panel even to avoid wasting fabric. Press each seam towards the darker strip, always ironing on the right side of the fabric.

6. Make two complete panels of eight colors, lightest to darkest, and join them, matching the darkest strip to the lightest, making a strip panel of 16 colors.

7. Trim off the uneven edge of the panel, using a rotary cutter and gridded ruler. Line up the horizontal lines on your ruler to match the seams in the panel to make sure you are cutting an accurate straight line (Figure 9-4).

Placement of
cut slices
for left half
of design:

¾″ (finishes to
¼″): 21 slices (rows
1, 2, 3, 9, 10, 11, 12,
13, 14, 15, plus 1
center strip)

cut 1″ (finishes to
½″): 6 slices (rows
4, 8, 16)

cut 1¼″ (finishes to
¾″): 6 slices (rows
5, 7, 17)

cut 1½″ (finishes to
1″): 4 slices (rows 6,
18)

Figure 9-3. Chart for panel colors A–H, and for design layout, strips 1–18.

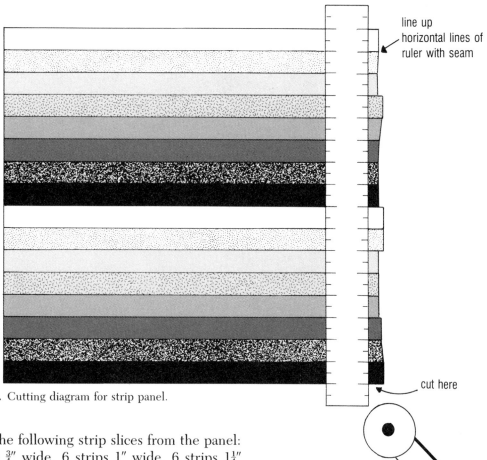

line up
horizontal lines of
ruler with seam

cut here

Figure 9-4. Cutting diagram for strip panel.

8. Cut the following strip slices from the panel: 21 strips $\frac{3}{4}''$ wide, 6 strips $1''$ wide, 6 strips $1\frac{1}{4}''$ wide, and 4 strips $1\frac{1}{2}''$ wide. Every fourth or fifth cut, line up the seams with the horizontal ruler lines again. It may be necessary to trim a thin wedge from the panel to straighten the edge.

On a flat surface, arrange the cut strips into the design, following the chart in Figure 9-3.

9. On the shiny side of the freezer paper, draw a rectangle the size of the center portion of your design ($17'' \times 14''$) Use a pencil or an extra fine point permanent marking pen to draw on the shiny surface. Mark the vertical and horizontal center lines, and then add lines in both directions every few inches to create a grid. These lines will be your stitching guides.

10. Start your design with the $\frac{3}{4}''$ center strip. Begin by carefully folding each color in the strip exactly in half and pinching the fold on either edge to make a small line across the color. This will be the "match point" to position the next two

strips accurately. When you have marked the halfway point of each color in this way, carefully fold the strip in half lengthwise, and match the fold to the center line on the freezer paper. Place a few pins horizontally to hold the first strip in place on the freezer paper. It is vitally important to get this first strip positioned correctly, since every other strip will be matched to it. If you have sewn exact $\frac{1}{4}''$ seams, the seam line on the first, or lightest color (A) should be at the upper edge of the rectangle and the bottom seam of color F should be at the bottom line of the rectangle (Figure 9-5). If your strip is slightly longer or shorter, adjust your rectangle to fit.

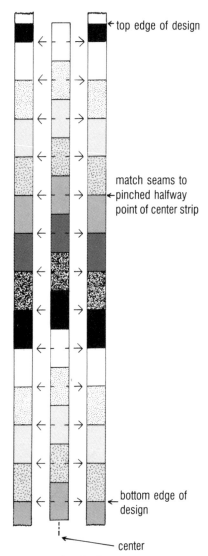

top edge of design

match seams to
pinched halfway
point of center strip

bottom edge of
design

center

Figure 9-5. Layout detail, showing arrangement of strips.

11. Sew the ends of a $\frac{3}{4}''$ strip together, right sides facing, the lightest color A to the darkest color H, to form a "loop." Use a stitch ripper to pull out the seam at the other side of color H so this strip now begins with H, the darkest color, instead of A, the lightest. Press the new seam, and repeat this process with another $\frac{3}{4}''$ strip.

12. *Top* pressed-piecing will be used for sewing this strip. With right sides together, moving down half a color, match the seam lines in one of these new $\frac{3}{4}''$ strips with the pinch marks on the left hand edge of the center strip. Match every seam with a pinchmark and pin in place on the freezer paper. At the upper edge of the rectangle, you should now have the half-way point of

color H, and at the bottom edge, the half-way point of color F (refer to Figure 9-5). Be sure to position the pins horizontally, since you will be sewing over them. When the second strip is in position, turn your work so that the seam is on the right, and using extra small stitches, sew the two strips together, through the paper.

13. Remove the pins and open out the strip. Finger press. Don't iron at this point, or you will lose all the pinchmarks on the other edge of the center strip.

14. Use the second "looped" strip and match it in the same way to the right hand edge of the center strip. Move down half a color, as before, and pin carefully through both fabric seams and paper, matching every seam to a pinch mark.

15. When this strip is pinned in place, turn the paper over and stitch this second seam from the back, using *under* pressed-piecing. Sew with $\frac{1}{4}''$ seam allowance, using the previous stitching line as your guide. This will give you a perfectly straight narrow strip on the front. If your presser foot is not exactly $\frac{1}{4}''$ from the needle, you can stitch a slightly wider or narrower seam; just be sure to use the same seam allowance every time. The finished size of your piece will vary with any change in seam allowance.

16. Turn to the front, remove the pins and press using a pressing cloth to cover the freezer paper. Be careful that your hot iron does not touch the shiny surface of the freezer paper or it will stick. Try to press only the seam, making sure the strips are fully open. It is easy to distort a strip as you iron to the paper so use the grid lines as guides. The strips should stick to the freezer paper and stay in position.

17. Make loops with two more $\frac{3}{4}''$ strips, then pull out the seams so each strip starts with color H. Press. Drop each strip down half a color and match the seams to the seams of the center strip. Refer again to Figure 9-2. Carefully pin each seam in place through the paper. Turn the paper over and sew from the back, using the previous seam line as your guide. Remove the pins and press the strips carefully onto the freezer paper. Use a pressing cloth to avoid scorching your work.

18. Following the graph, make two more $\frac{3}{4}''$ strips into loops, pulling out the seam after color G. Drop each strip half a color and carefully pin every seam in place, matching the seams to the strips on either side of the center. Sew from the back, remove the pins and press, as before. Place a ruler on the front of the work, matching the grid lines, to make sure the strips are going on straight.

19. Next, make loops from two 1″ strips so that each begins with color G. Sew, pull out the previous seam and press as before. Drop each strip down half a color, matching seams across the design. The seams in alternate strips will match. Pin, sew from the back, and press both these new strips.

20. Loop and sew two $1\frac{1}{4}''$ strips so that color F appears at the top. Pin in place and this time sew from the right side of the fabric. Press.

21. Continue looping strips to get the correct color at the top, sewing strips to the pattern, following the graph for the correct strip width and colors. Larger width strips are sewn from the front of the design. To get accurate narrow strips, sew $\frac{3}{4}''$ strips from the back, using the previous stitch line as your guide. When you add the first $\frac{3}{4}''$ strip in a sequence, sew that first seam from the front of the design. All the other $\frac{3}{4}''$ strips that are added to the first will be sewn from the back, including the final seam when a wider strip is added to the last $\frac{3}{4}''$ strip. Follow the pattern carefully, and be sure to move the colors up when the design bends, beginning with strip #13. Carefully iron each strip to the freezer paper after it is sewn, checking the gridlines for accuracy.

22. When the entire design has been sewn, mark the rectangle lines on the fabric and run a line of small stitches just outside the rectangle, very close to the edge, to hold all the seams in place. Add $\frac{1}{4}''$ seam allowance on all sides and trim.

23. Remove the freezer paper by pulling it away from the fabric gently, being careful not to stretch or break your stitches. Use a stitch ripper to remove small stubborn pieces.

24. For the border: cut 2 strips $\frac{3}{4}''$ wide of color A; cut 2 strips 1″ wide, of color E; and 2 strips $1\frac{1}{4}''$ wide of color H. Sew two panels of colors A, E, and H. Press from the right side, with seams towards the darkest fabric. Sew the border to the quilt, mitering corners (see Chapter 8). A fourth, wider border can be added if desired.

25. Baste, quilt, and bind. Because of the many seams, it is impractical to hand quilt a bargello design in the body of the quilt. Use smoke-colored "invisible" nylon thread. Machine quilting can be "in-the-ditch" on all the vertical seams, or follow the undulating line of the pattern and quilt "in-the-ditch" horizontally. Another option would be to machine quilt "free-hand" across the piece.

26. Sign and date your quilt.

Peace Lily #1
by Eileen Sullivan
(Color Plate 36)

Eileen's original design (Figure 9-6) and foundation use are both innovative. Her technical challenge was to design a quilt that could be pieced on paper, while allowing variations within each unit. Since there is no repeat, each section had to be dealt with and designed individually. Her use of freezer paper foundation piecing combines the benefits of *under* pressed piecing and string piecing as well as single foundation piecing to make possible designs that otherwise might be unmanageable.

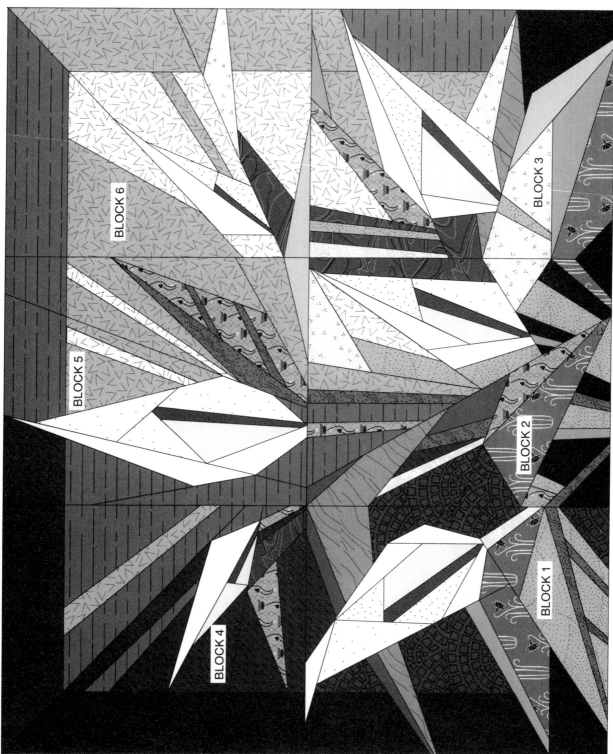

Figure 9-6. *Peace Lily #1 layout.*

Eileen feels that the merits of her method of freezer paper foundation piecing are:

1. Freedom to piece very strange or difficult angles and sharp points precisely.
2. No need for individual templates.
3. Easy color and fabric changes.

4. Freezer paper foundations serve as both a master template and as a fabric stabilizer when dealing with bias situations.
5. There is no critical seam allowance to deal with when piecing. Using the under foundation method, the drawn line is easy to follow and is exactly where she wants it.

She sees the disadvantages as:

1. It does not provide for economical use of fabric. This is not a technique for the "faint of heart" who worry about wasting fabric.
2. Learning to sew "inside out" with the *under* foundation method takes practice.
3. This type of designing requires careful planning and a system for keeping track of fabrics in a letter or number code.
4. It is messy, with a lot of trimmings to clean up and paper to remove.

Quilt Size: 24″ × 20″

Block Size: 8″ × 10″ (6 blocks)

Materials

¼ yd of six fabrics ranging from black to light grey in smooth gradation.

¼ yd or less of ten green fabrics ranging from deep forest green, through jade or teal, to lighter greens; appropriate prints and solids

Small amounts of four shades of cream to white for flowers.

Scraps of mid-tone tan or tan/green for centers of flowers, appropriate print

Graph paper; carbon paper; colored pencils

Freezer paper

Backing fabric; batting; binding

Construction Directions

1. Organize the fabrics by color values, from dark to light in each color. Assign a code number to each (Figure 9-7) Each block is made up of several "sections." Each piece in the section is numbered with the sewing sequence as well as the fabric to be used (Figure 9-8).

Figure 9-8. Eileen's color and piecing plan.

2. The patterns have been reduced to fit onto the pages of the book. You may use them this size, which will reduce the size of your finished quilt, or you may enlarge them to their original size by photocopying them with a 125% enlargement.

3. Trace each block from the book on graph paper, or use the enlarged photocopy of each block. Transfer all fabric code and sewing sequence numbers in each section (Figures 9-9 to 9-14).

(text continues on p. 114)

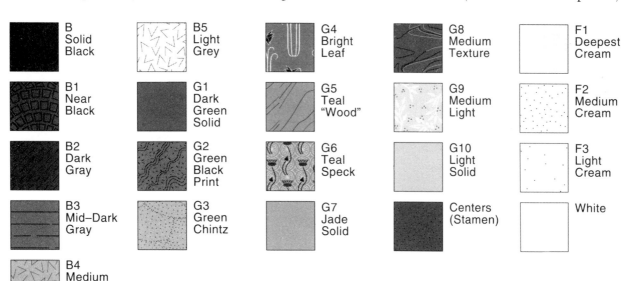

B Solid Black	B5 Light Grey	G4 Bright Leaf	G8 Medium Texture	F1 Deepest Cream
B1 Near Black	G1 Dark Green Solid	G5 Teal "Wood"	G9 Medium Light	F2 Medium Cream
B2 Dark Gray	G2 Green Black Print	G6 Teal Speck	G10 Light Solid	F3 Light Cream
B3 Mid–Dark Gray	G3 Green Chintz	G7 Jade Solid	Centers (Stamen)	White
B4 Medium Gray				

Figure 9-7. Color chart.

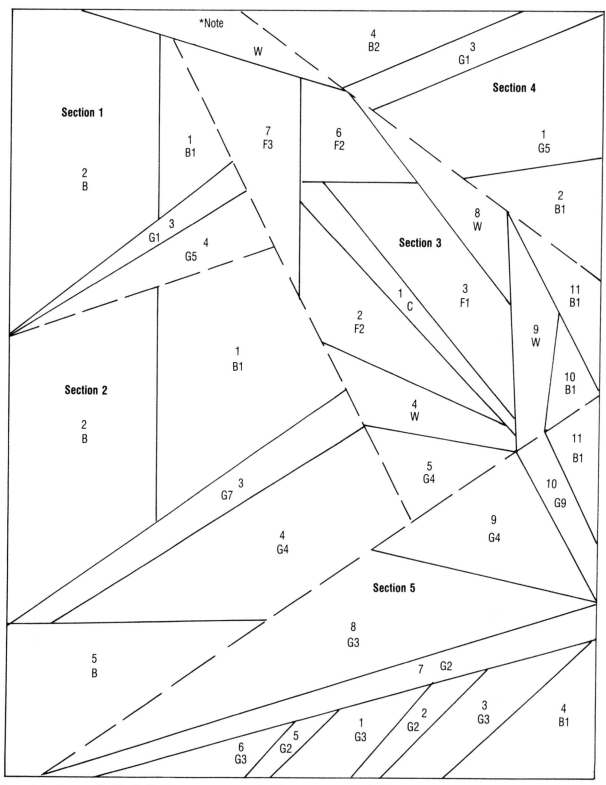

Figure 9-9. Pattern for Block #1. Piece sections 1 and 2, then join. Piece and add section 3. *Note:* add * piece. Piece and add sections 4 and 5.

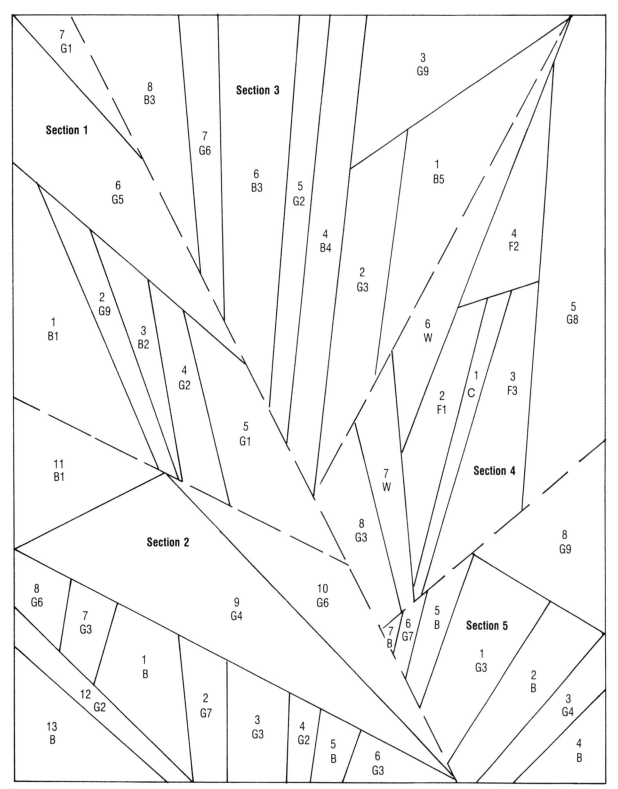

Figure 9-10. Pattern for Block #2. Piece sections 1 and 2; join. Piece sections 3, 4 and 5; join 3, 4 and 5. Then assemble 1/2 and 3/4/5.

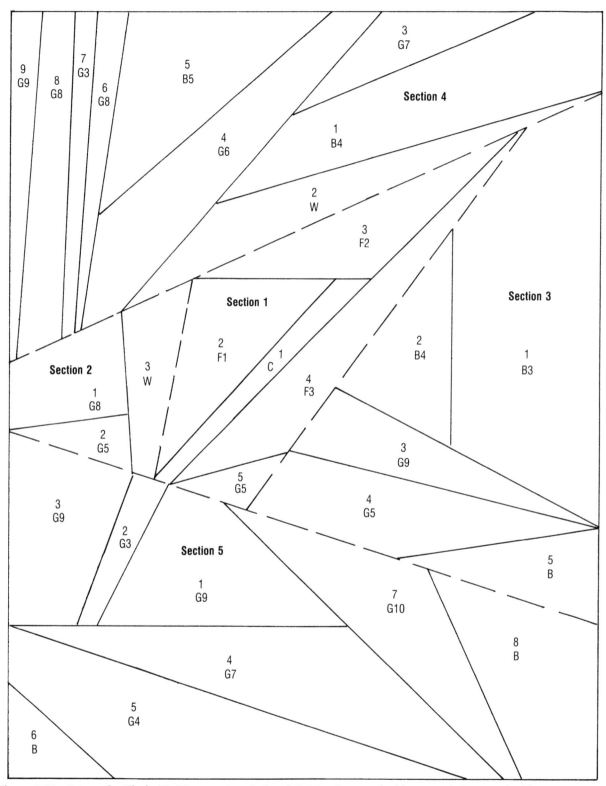

Figure 9-11. Pattern for Block #3. Piece sections 1, 2 and 3; join. Piece and add section 4. Piece and add section 5.

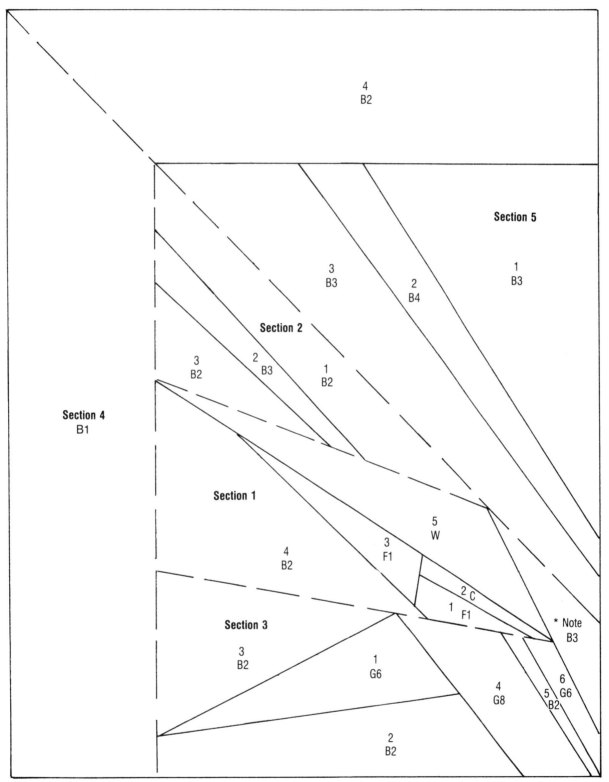

Figure 9-12. Pattern for Block #4. Piece and join sections 1, 2 and 3. *Note:* add * piece. Add section 4, then piece and add section 5.

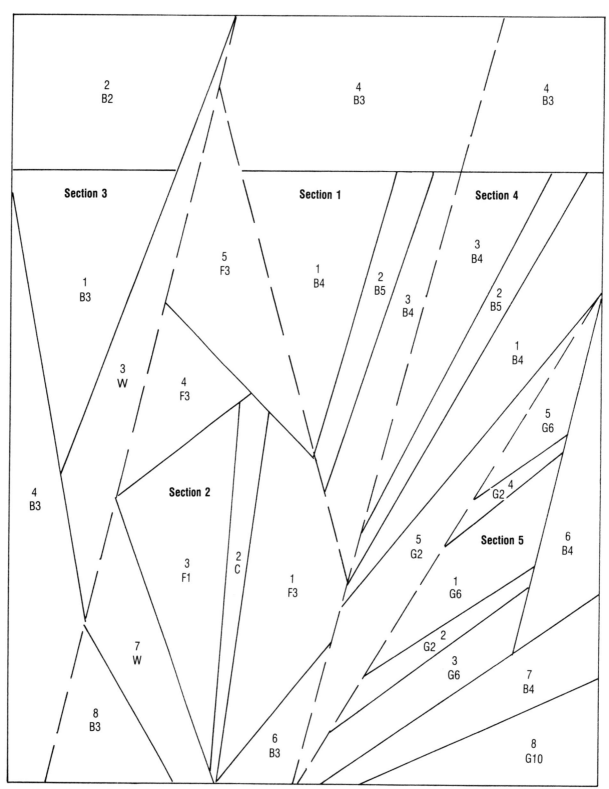

Figure 9-13. Pattern for Block #5. Piece sections 1 and 2; join. Piece section 3 and add. Piece sections 4 and 5, join. Add 1/2/3 to 4/5 to complete.

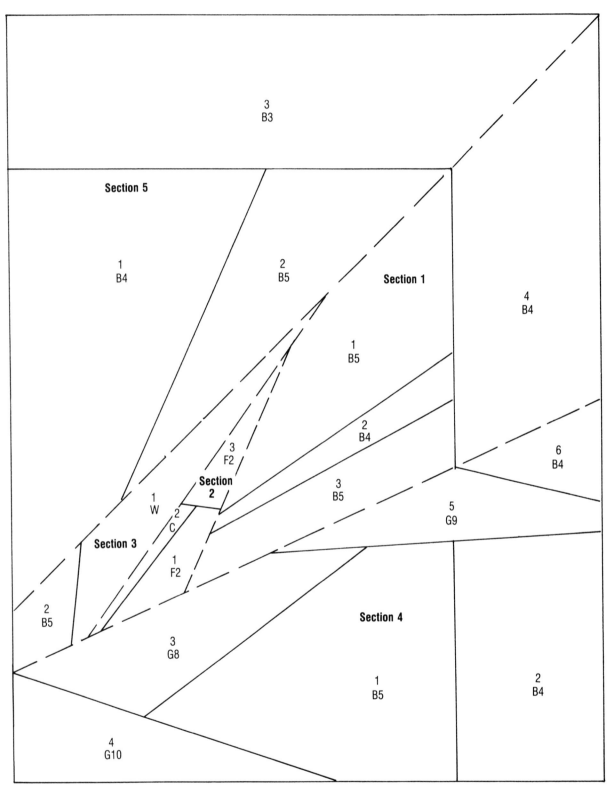

Figure 9-14. Pattern for Block #6. Piece sections 1 and 2, then join sections. Piece section 3, then add to 1 and 2. Complete sections 4 and 5, then join to complete the block.

4. To copy the designs onto freezer paper: Layer the carbon paper, carbon side up, the freezer paper shiny side up, and the drawing on top, right side up. Tape this stack to a sheet of cardboard (Figure 9-15). Trace all the lines carefully, using the broken line to indicate where the block will be cut apart. The designs will be transferred to the dull side of the freezer paper. This transfer method avoids the mirror image that would have resulted if you had traced the designs directly onto freezer paper.

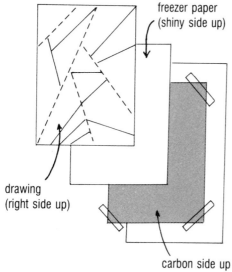

Figure 9-15. Tracing process to avoid mirror image.

5. Working on one block at a time, after all lines are traced, trim away the excess freezer paper, along the edges of the block. Using colored pencils, add several reference marks along each long dotted line which divides the sections to aid in reconnecting. Note the fabric to be used for each area, either by number code, or by taping on a small piece for reference. Once the units are cut apart, it will be difficult to be sure of what you are working on without identification. Cut apart the sections of the block on the dotted lines.

General sewing directions: Do not try to cut shapes or sizes to cover an area. It is best to work with a larger piece, to insure adequate coverage when flipped, and trimmed after sewing. Eileen often pre-cuts "fat quarters" from her yardage, to have manageable pieces to use in the piecing process.

Although freezer paper helps to hold bias edges in place, whenever possible, try to add a straight grain piece to any obvious bias edge. And always try to keep a straight grain, preferably a lengthwise grain at the outer edges of the block and the quilt. Careful control while piecing will help to avoid problems when the foundation is removed later.

Each section of each block is different, and the sewing sequence must always proceed according to the pattern. Usually the #1 piece is the innermost and is subsequently crossed by others. The sequence for adding pieces is indicated on each section. In a few areas a * piece is indicated. This is a piece which crosses over more than one section. Complete the required sections, join together, and then add the * piece.

6. Beginning with Section 1 of Block 1, lay a piece of fabric larger than the area to be covered with the wrong side against the shiny side of the freezer paper and press in place (Figure 9-16). Place the fabric for the next piece on top of the first, right sides together (Figure 9-17). To assure that you have enough fabric to cover the area once it is sewn and flipped, hold the section up to the light from the drawn side. Alternately, you can pin along the sewing line, flip the piece open

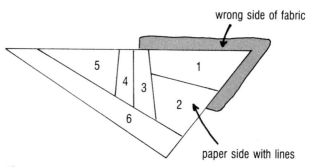

Figure 9-16. First piece of fabric ironed onto shiny side of freezer paper.

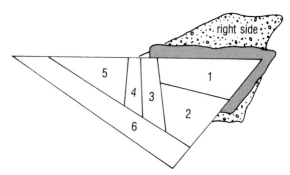

Figure 9-17. Second piece of fabric in place, right sides of fabric together.

and check that it covers the space adequately. You need enough fabric to provide a $\frac{1}{4}''$ seam allowance within the section and up to $\frac{1}{2}''$ seam allowance on the outside edges.

7. Turn the paper over, with the drawn side towards you, and stitch on the line, 2 or 3 stitches before it begins through the seam allowance area outside the section. Use a smaller than usual stitch length (Figure 9-18). Open the piece and check that the fabric covers the area. You can "rough cut" to get rid of excess fabric at this point if you wish.

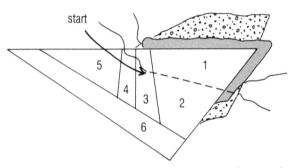

Figure 9-18. Stitching first pieces. Start a few stitches *before* indicated seam line.

8. Fold the freezer paper back along the stitched line, first freeing the fabric from the paper as needed, and trim the seam allowance to a scant $\frac{1}{4}''$ (Figure 9-19). It is essential to trim at this point since if there is excess fabric in the seam allowance, it will be trapped after the next strip is attached. If fabrics have a possibility of "shadowing," trim the darker fabric slightly smaller than the lighter.

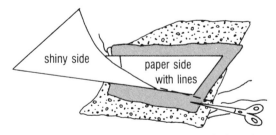

Figure 9-19. Trim excess seam allowance *before* flipping and ironing in place.

9. Open the pieces and press along the sewn line, first from the fabric side, for a crisp seam, and then from the paper side to insure that the freezer paper is firmly secured (Figure 9-20). Note: Place a clean sheet of newsprint on the ironing board to protect against possible transfer of the carbon lines. Change it as needed.

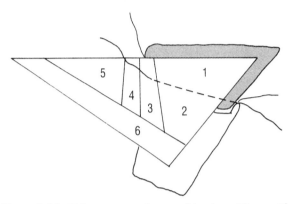

Figure 9-20. Fabric open and pressed in place. Wrong side of fabric will adhere to shiny side of freezer paper.

10. Continue following the sewing sequence, until all the pieces in the section have been sewn in place and all the areas are covered (Figure 9-21). Carefully trim the excess fabric from the outside edges of the section leaving a $\frac{1}{4}''$ seam allowance beyond the edge of the freezer paper.

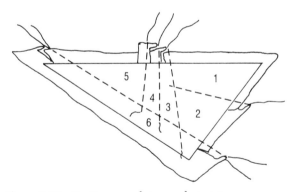

Figure 9-21. Section complete, ready to trim.

11. Piece the next sections for Block 1. Sections are joined together in order, as noted on each pattern, to complete the block. Keep in mind

your assembly plan so that you have long straight seams and do not end up in a pivoting situation. Although we do this frequently in regular piecing, it is difficult with freezer paper in place.

Place the fabric sides of two sections to be joined together, using your reference marks as guides. Align and pin the marks and any critical joins. Pin along the remaining edges of the freezer paper, checking both sides to be sure you are on the "sewing line." Sew right at the edge of the paper. Press the seam allowance towards the side of the least resistance with the fewest intersecting seams, unless color and shadowing is a problem. If necessary, the seams can be pressed in one direction, pivoting to the other side where needed. Press from both sides for a crisp seam (Figure 9-22).

Figure 9-22. Reverse of quilt top, showing pressed seams.

12. Complete each block in a similar manner and join the blocks in rows, matching crosspoints. You can remove some of the paper as each block is completed, but do not remove paper near the edges until the blocks have been joined, as the foundation is the seam allowance stitching line. Eileen uses tweezers, and runs the dull end up under the areas first, to free the fabric so that the paper comes off in large pieces.

13. Baste, quilt, and bind. This was machine quilted "in the ditch" around the flowers, stems, leaves, and background color changes. Additional lines in the flowers and veins in the leaves were quilted, following the general contours of the shapes. The open spaces of the background were quilted with randomly placed and spaced lines roughly parallel to the ditch and radiating outward toward the edges.

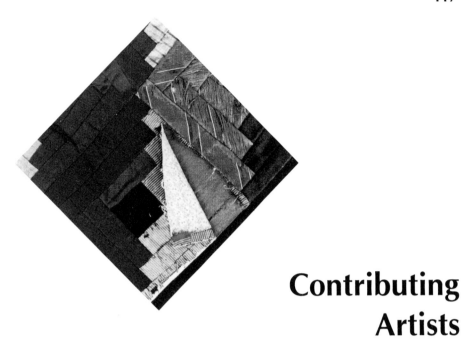

Contributing Artists

Jennifer Amor, Columbia, S.C., is a professional quiltmaker working in non-traditional techniques and wearable art. A self-taught quilter with a background in art and journalism, she has been exploring bargello designs since 1982. She teaches quiltmaking throughout the United States and she has worked as an artist-in-residence in South Carolina schools for the last five years. She is the author of *Flavor Quilts For Kids To Make*, a book about teaching children to make memory quilts. Her work has won many awards, has been published in quilt magazines, books, and calendars.

Barbara Elwell, Raleigh, N.C., is a self-taught quiltmaker with a background in clothing construction and other needlearts. While living in Thailand, she became interested in the handwoven ikat that is a traditional village cloth and uses it extensively to reinterpret familiar quilt designs. Her work has won awards and been exhibited nationally, and is in several private and corporate collections. She has written articles for leading quilt magazines.

Janet Elwin, Damariscotta, Maine, has been exploring and teaching quiltmaking since 1973. She was one of the founders of the New England Quilters Guild, and during her term as president, initiated the plans for the establishment of the New England Quilt Museum; this became a

reality in 1987. Her work has won many awards and been extensively published in leading magazines. Janet is known for using the hexagon shape to interpret her ideas into colorful and intriguing quilts and wall hangings. She is the author of *Hexagon Magic*, two self-published booklets, and quilt and patchwork clothing patterns.

Caryl Bryer Fallert, Oswego, Ill., is known for her unusual and striking works of fabric art. Formally trained in design, color, and studio painting, she found that fabric as an artistic medium best expressed her personal vision, after discovering the tactile qualities of fabric and the unlimited color range made possible by hand dyeing. On the back of most of her quilts, Caryl honors the anonymous quiltmakers of the past by piecing in an adaptation of a traditional block. Her award winning quilts and art to wear have been seen in numerous national and international exhibits and are in a number of private and corporate collections.

Mary Golden lives in New Hampton, N.H. in the winter and in Gloucester, Mass. during the summer. She has been quilting for 20 years and is a nationally known quiltmaking teacher. Her award winning quilts have been featured in quilt magazines, calendars, and books. Mary is especially known for her use of Log Cabin, Pineapple, and Kaleidoscope patterns. She is the author of

The Friendship Quilt Book and publishes papers for use with foundation piecing.

Debbie Hall, Cincinnati, Ohio, is a self-taught quilter with a Fine Arts degree. Her interest in mathematics and experience with computers as a systems analyst led her to working out faster and more accurate ways of piecing quilts. Her interests have evolved from a focus on color, fabric and pattern in creating prize-winning quilts, to active involvement in building an international community through quiltmaking. She has travelled to Kharkov in the Ukraine as part of a sister-city delegation and is working to bring two Ukrainian quilt artists to Cincinnati.

June Ryker, Lakewood, Colorado, specializes in original and innovative Log Cabin designs. Her award-winning quilts have been widely exhibited and published in quilting books and magazines. She teaches and lectures nationally and internationally; she designs and markets many of her own patterns. June was recently inducted into the Colorado Quilting Council's Hall of Fame.

Dory Sandon, North Palm Beach, Florida, is a studio quilter who has won national awards for her quilts. Her work is exhibited throughout the United States in art galleries and museums, and is in private and corporate collections from Florida to Canada. A former hand-piecer, Dory credits working on foundations for making it feasible for her to machine-piece.

Sonja Shogren, Raleigh, N.C., is originally from Switzerland, and has a degree in Architectural Interior Design from Zurich. She has been a quiltmaker for fifteen years, and has won awards in quilt shows and galleries, locally and nationally. She has always been a precision piecer; her special interest now lies with miniaturized Log Cabin patterns, ranging from traditional to innovative sets.

Eileen Sullivan, Columbia, S.C., has a degree in Art Education, and taught art in public schools for eight years. She began making traditional quilts in 1979, and started designing creatively in 1983. She is primarily interested in innovative design and exploration of techniques. Her award winning quilts have been exhibited throughout

the country and are in several private and corporate collections. She has been published in quilt magazines and calendars, and also lectures and judges quilt shows.

Cheryl Trostrud-White, Calabasas, Calif., uses her quiltmaking skills for both quilts and clothing. Her garments have been exhibited in three Fairfield fashion shows. She says that her work has been influenced by three artistic impulses from her childhood: a love of geometry inherited from her father's intricate tile compositions, a love of the fiber arts from her Norwegian ancestry, and a love of music that results in orchestrated color schemes.

Julia Wernicke, Pensacola, Florida, is an accomplished embroiderer and an inveterate quilt collector. She interprets traditional designs and often duplicates worn antique quilts. She particularly enjoys sharing quilts with children and non-quilting members of the community.

Joann Wilson, Pensacola, Florida, came to quiltmaking with a background of a wide variety of needlework. She is admired for working through a technique until she masters it, and for finishing what she starts.

Jane Hall and **Dixie Haywood** are self-taught quilters who are known for adapting traditional designs using contemporary techniques and innovative approaches. Their award-winning quilts have been exhibited throughout the country, and are in private and corporate collections. Both have been teaching and judging quiltmaking for many years and have a commitment to encouraging students to use their skills creatively in ways that will make quilts uniquely their own. Longtime friends, they have collaborated previously on *Perfect Pineapples* (C & T Publishing, 1989). Dixie is also the author of two books on contemporary crazy quilting and has written extensively for magazines. Jane is a certified appraiser for old and new quilts. Jane lives in Raleigh, N.C., with her husband, Bob. They are the parents of six children, and have three grandchildren. Dixie lives in Pensacola, Fla., with her husband, Bob. They are the parents of a daughter, two sons and two grandchildren.

Resources

The following companies have products useful for piecing on foundations. Please enclose a self-addressed stamped envelope when inquiring.

Bonesteel's Hardware and Quilt Corner
150 White Street
Hendersonville, North Carolina 28739
"Grid-Grip," gridded freezer paper; printed paper foundations for Pineapple blocks.

D. A. Brinkman
154 Gordon Drive
Spartanburg, South Carolina 29301
Printed paper foundations for Pineapple blocks, several small sizes.

C & T Publishing
5021 Blum Road, #1
Martinez, California 94553
Printed paper foundations for Perfect Pineapples, 6 inch and 9 inch blocks.

Mary Golden
Box 333
New Hampton, NH 13256
Printed paper foundations for many traditional patterns including Ocean Waves, Alphabet, Building, as well as Pineapple, Log Cabin and Kaleidoscope; several sizes for all patterns.

Lynn Graves
Little Foot Ltd.
605 Bledsoe, NW
Albuquerque, NM 87107
Printed paper foundations for Pineapple, various sizes of Log Cabin blocks, Flying Geese and Braids. Design sheets for Log Cabin and Pineapple patterns.

Hahner/Griffin Studios
PO Box 178
Fanwood, New Jersey 07023
Printed paper foundations for Kaleidoscope blocks, several sizes.

Jane McQuade
19 Halsey Drive
Smithfield, RI 02917
Printed paper foundations for Pineapple, Flying Geese and Geese in the Cabin patterns, several sizes.

Paper Pieces
P.O. Box 2931
Redmond, WA 90703-2931
Papers and patterns for single foundation piecing, several shapes and sizes.

Patchwork Stamps
6438 Covington Road
Fort Wayne, Indiana 46804
Printed papers and stamped muslin squares for foundation piecing, including Sunburst, Card Trick, Spinning Star, and many others; various sizes.

Quilt Arts
4114 Minstell Lane
Fairfax, Virginia 22033
    Rubber stamps for marking Log Cabin and
    Pineapple patterns on fabric or paper,
    several sizes.

Bonnie Jean Rosenbaum
3513 Smith SE
Albuquerque, New Mexico 87106
    Printed paper foundations for small Flying
    Geese, Pineapple, Log Cabin and Braid
    patterns.

June Ryker
The Quilted Lady
1464 South Ward Street
Lakewood, CO 80228
    Innovative Log Cabin patterns, using
    foundations.

Sonja Shogren
SCS Designs
1815 Falls Church Road
Raleigh, NC 27609
    Printed paper patterns for miniature ($1\frac{1}{2}''$
    and $1\frac{7}{8}''$ block) Log Cabins with five logs.

Small Patches
12715 Warwick Boulevard
Newport News, Virginia 23606
    Rubber stamps for small blocks such as
    House, Tree, Sailboat, Basket, as well as
    Log Cabins and other traditional patterns.

Eileen Sullivan
The Designers Workshop
P.O. Box 23153
Columbia, SC 29224
    Patterns for innovative wall quilts
    including a larger Peace Lily, using
    freezer paper

The Stencil Company
P.O Box 1218
Williamsville, NY 14221
    Plastic stencils for marking foundations
    with selected June Ryker patterns, to
    include Fantasy Too.

Bibliography

Beyer, Jinny. *The Quilter's Album of Blocks & Borders*. McLean, Va: EPM Publications, Inc., 1980.

Brackman, Barbara. *An Encyclopedia of Pieced Patterns*. Lawrence, Ks: Flower Publishing, 1979 and 1984.

Brackman, Barbara. *Clues in the Calico*. McLean, Va: EPM Publications, Inc, 1989.

Bonesteel, Georgia. *New Ideas for Lap Quilting*. Birmingham, Al: Oxmoor House, 1987.

Campbell-Harding, Valerie. *Strip Patchwork*. New York: Dover Publications, Inc., 1983.

Drellich, Karen Kinney. *Yvonne Porcella: Nurse turned Fabric Designer*. Peoria, Il: PJS Publications, Inc., Sew News, No.30, March 1985, pp 62–63.

Elwin, Janet. *Hexagon Magic*. McLean, Va: E.P.M. Publications, Inc., 1986. *Celebration Quilts*, Damariscotta, Me: self-published, 1989. *Ode to Grandmother*, Damariscotta, Me: self-published, 1991.

Fairfield, Helen. *Patchwork from Mosaics*. New York: Arco Publishing Co., 1985.

Fallert, Caryl Bryer. *String Piecing*. Paducah, Ky: American Quilter, Vol VI, No. 3. Fall 1990, pp 14–21. *Creative String Piecing*. Wheatridge, Co: Quilter's Newsletter, No. 195, Sept. 1987, pp 23–25.

Fanning, Robbie and Tony. *The Complete Book of Machine Quilting*. Radnor, Pa: Chilton Book Company, 1980.

Golden, Mary. *The Friendship Quilt Book*. Dublin, N.H.: Yankee Publishing Inc., 1985.

Hall, Debbie. *A Pieceful Revolution*. Paducah, Ky: American Quilter, Vol IV, No. 1. Spring 1988, pp 49–52.

Hall, Jane and Haywood, Dixie. *Perfect Pineapples*. Martinez, Ca: C & T Publishing, 1989.

Hall, Carrie A., and Kretsinger, Rose G. *The Romance of the Patchwork Quilt*. New York: Bonanza Books, 1935.

Haywood, Dixie. *Crazy Quilting Patchwork*. New York: Dover Publications, Inc., 1986.

Haywood, Dixie. *Quick Crazy Quilt Patchwork*. New York: Dover Publications, Inc., 1992.

Herlan, Tess. *Patterns for Paper Piecing*. Redmond, Wa: Paper Pieces, 1990.

Leman, Bonnis and Martin, Judy. *Log Cabin Quilts*. Denver, Co: M.Q.M. Publishing Co., 1980.

Liddell, Jill and Watanabe, Yuko. *Japanese Quilts*. New York: E.P. Dutton, 1988.

Mathieson, Judy. *Mariner's Compass*. Martinez, Ca: C & T Publishing, 1987.

Montano, Judith. *The Crazy Quilt Handbook*. Martinez, Ca: C & T Publishing, 1986.

Montano, Judith. *Crazy Quilt Odyssey*. Martinez, Ca: C & T Publishing, 1991.

Ouchi, Hajame. *Japanese Optical and Geometrical Art*. New York: Dover Publications, Inc., 1977.

Porcella, Yvonne. *Pieced Clothing Variations*. Modesto, Ca: Porcella Studios, 1981.

Puckett, Marjorie. *String Quilts 'n Things*. Orange, Ca: Orange Patchwork Publishers, 1979.

Rae, Janet. *Quilts of the British Isles*. New York: E.P. Dutton, 1987.

Rose, Helen Whitson. *Quilting with Strips and Strings*. New York: Dover Publications, Inc., 1983.

Ryker, June. *A Genius Shines Through/Bloomin' Logs*. New Milford, Pa: Chitra Publications, Traditional Quiltworks #16. *The Great American Classics, Log Cabin: an Update*. Wheatridge, Co: Quilter's Newsletter, No. 201, pp. 33–39.

Shirer, Marie and Brackman, Barbara. *Creature Comforts*. Lombard, Il: Wallace-Homestead, 1986. No longer in print.

Von Gwinner, Schnuppe. *The History of the Patchwork Quilt*. Westchester, Pa: Schiffer Publishing Co., 1988.

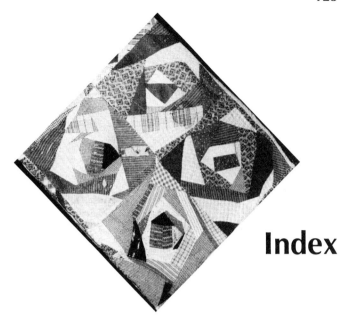

Index